"For decades, Christian thinkers have garnered tremendous gains in defending the existence of God. With important exceptions, the same cannot be said about defending God's goodness in light of biblical texts that seem to say otherwise. Accordingly, I am thrilled about the release of Tingblad and McDowell's stunning book *Why Did God Do That?* While well organized and accessible, this book is deep, thorough, and carefully researched. I learned a lot from reading it. Two things stood out to me: First, though other books have addressed particular issues, I know of no book that brings together all the main problems in one place. This alone makes the book invaluable. Second, by emphasizing God's patience, his desire that all be saved, his constant warnings of judgment, his holiness, and the severity of human sin and depravity, Tingblad and McDowell argue convincingly not that God is good in spite of these texts; rather, he is good within them. There is no book like this one. I could not recommend it more highly."

—**J.P. Moreland,** Distinguished Professor of Philosophy,
Talbot School of Theology, Biola University, and
author of *A Simple Guide to Experience Miracles*

"Through the centuries, the Christian community has been prompted by varying cultures to respond to the questions of an all-powerful God dealing with the brokenness of a fallen world. Fortunately, the truth of God's Word stands strong as a foundation to understand the reality of a loving and good God. But how can the church respond when Scripture itself seems to present God in a negative light? Matthew Tingblad and Josh McDowell offer very thorough encouragement in *Why Did God Do That?* This book provides ample evidence that God does not require us to blindly trust in his goodness when faced with Bible difficulties. Truly, the good news of God's grace through Jesus Christ bursts forth in the midst of this discussion as a source of great hope and inspiration. Knowing God's holiness and our sin against him, we should be amazed at his mercy, not judgment. Even so, God does not delight in judgment, but desires all people to be saved. *Why Did God Do That?* will be a useful reference tool for all believers as they share, with conviction, that God is consistently good and just."

—**Miles McPherson,** senior ~~pastor~~ f the Rock Church,
Diego, California

"Violence in the Old Testament. Misogyny. Hell. These are topics many Christians would shy away from or try to dismiss with a quick answer. Instead, Tingblad and McDowell acknowledge the real challenge these topics pose—and yet boldly proclaim that Christianity has the resources to demonstrate God's goodness. This is a nuanced, well-balanced, and exceedingly strong case for our good God."

—**Lee Strobel,** *New York Times* bestselling author and founding director of the Lee Strobel Center for Evangelism and Applied Apologetics, Colorado Christian University

"Although I am (obviously) biased, I thoroughly enjoyed this book. Tingblad and McDowell do not shy away from the thorniest ethical issues in the Old Testament. Through extensive research, reflection, and personal examples, they offer insights that will help both believers and skeptics make sense of the claim that God is not good."

—**Sean McDowell, PhD,** professor of apologetics at Biola University, and author or coauthor of many books, including *A Rebel's Manifesto*

"What Tingblad and McDowell have done in this book is absolutely fearless. They've pulled no punches and addressed hard questions head-on. Whether you are struggling with some difficult theological doubts yourself, or you want to be better prepared to talk about your faith with someone who is not a follower of Jesus, Tingblad and McDowell have paved the way for you in the most delightfully accessible and theologically rich manner. This apologetic work is perfectly timed for a society struggling to navigate numerous challenges to God and his Word."

—**Adam Griffin,** lead pastor, Eastside Community Church in Dallas, Texas, coauthor of *Family Discipleship*, and host of the *Family Discipleship Podcast*

MATTHEW TINGBLAD
with JOSH McDOWELL

Why Did
GOD
Do That?

HARVEST HOUSE PUBLISHERS
EUGENE, OREGON

Cover design by Brock Book Design Co., Charles Brock

Cover images © Suraphol / Adobe Stock; gldburger / iStockphoto

Interior Design by Matt Shoemaker Design

For bulk, special sales, or ministry purchases, please call 1-800-547-8979.
Email: Customerservice@hhpbooks.com

This logo is a federally registered trademark of the Hawkins Children's LLC. Harvest House Publishers, Inc., is the exclusive licensee of this trademark.

Why Did God Do That?
Copyright © 2023 by Josh McDowell Ministry
Published by Harvest House Publishers
Eugene, Oregon 97408
www.harvesthousepublishers.com

ISBN 978-0-7369-8712-7 (pbk)
ISBN 978-0-7369-8713-4 (eBook)

Library of Congress Control Number: 2023932956

Printed in the United States of America

23 24 25 26 27 28 29 30 31 / BP / 10 9 8 7 6 5 4 3 2 1

To my parents, Tom and Linda:
You always strive to model the goodness of God for me.
Thank you.

Acknowledgments

Heavenly Father, I am amazed at your providence in bringing so many people together for the creation of this book.

Thank you for providing Tom Williams, who believed in this ambitious project and strengthened the manuscript with me. I learned so much working with him, and I don't think this book could have been published without his help.

Thank you for my friends Chad Hardin, Joel Novick, Taylor Skidmore, and Austin Woodruff, among others, for their encouragement during the entire writing (and rewriting) process.

Thank you for everyone on my team of ministry partners who have prayed for this book and supported me so that I could devote my time to research and writing.

Thank you for allowing me to be a part of Josh McDowell Ministry. What an honor to serve alongside Dave Bottorff, Duane and Genie Zook, Zack Wilson, and many others who have helped tremendously to make this book possible. I never knew serving you could be so fun and rewarding until joining the staff here.

Thank you, God, for bringing the right people to find this book. May the combined effort of everyone who helped with this project lead to moments of clarity and confidence that your Word never fails to reveal your goodness.

Contents

Preface:

The Trial of God Is
Now in Session

Today in the Western nations, God is on trial. The charges against him are multiple and include cruelty, insensitivity, severity, racism, sexism, favoritism, and abuse of power. Exhibit A in the trial is the Bible itself, which seems to provide smoking-gun evidence of these charges. It's not surprising that many atheists, agnostics, and other non-Christians are crying out for conviction. In fact, many Christians also wonder if there might not be some substance to these charges.

The purpose of this book is to defend and vindicate the goodness of God by looking hard at the passages in Scripture that seem to convey the opposite conclusion. In the pages that follow, we will take you on a journey from the hovels and palaces of Egypt to the battlefields of Canaan and even to the throne room of God. Not only will we show you reasons why God's actions achieve ultimate good, we will turn the idea of God's badness on its head. We will demonstrate that his every action is motivated by his holiness, his lovingkindness, his graciousness, his righteousness, and his deep and unfailing love for us.

Unless God is truly good, the Christian faith collapses. Christianity is based not only on the reality of God's existence but also on the reality of his goodness. We don't have to like everything God does any more than we like everything our doctor does to cure a deadly disease. But for our faith to rest firmly in him, we must be convinced of his goodness. The goodness of God is necessary in order for Christianity to make sense. After all, the word *gospel* means "good news," and it is good news because a good God has given us a way out of the finality of death and into a joyous life with him both now and forever.

We commend you skeptics and other non-Christian readers for taking the time to hear us out as you wrestle with these issues that trouble you. We encourage you to take these issues seriously. Turn the pages slowly. We recognize you have the freedom to believe whatever you want. But we hope our defenses and explanations of God's goodness will enable you to see him in a new and clarifying light.

Prayerfully yours,
Matthew Tingblad with Josh McDowell

1

Just How Good Is God?

Properly read, [the Bible] is the most potent
force for atheism ever conceived.[1]

—ISAAC ASIMOV

When we understand the greatness of God,
the stability of His character, the perfection of
His justice, the depth of His grace, the limitless
nature of His love, the wonder of His holiness,
and the sacrifice of His Son, it should not be
difficult for us to be moved greatly in our desire to
worship God, and worship Him passionately.[2]

—MICAH LANG

Many unbelievers claim that reading the Bible is what turned them to atheism. It might surprise you that we would open a book written to vindicate the goodness of God with such a lead sentence. But we wrote it because it's true. We have encountered numerous people and read many blogs and magazine articles by writers who were once Christians but turned away because they could not stomach the seemingly erratic nature and severity of God's judgments as recorded in the Bible.

For example, one woman who was raised a Christian decided to read her Bible while feeding her newborn daughter. She wrote of being disturbed by the Old Testament with its endless wars and wrath of God:

> Had the Bible always been so inconsistent, so violent, so sexist? Had it always needed so much adjustment to fit with my own sense of right and wrong? I tried to stretch my faith, twisting it like the rubber band I had looped through my buttonhole to give me a few more weeks in my pre-maternity jeans, but it didn't fit. I tried to ignore my questions and doubts as I had in the past, but there was a new question I could not ignore: What am I going to teach my daughter?

Her answer was to turn away from God and her church.[3]

A Christian blogger wrote of a recent discussion he had with a woman who was raised in a Christian family. She attended church all her life until she became an atheist in her twenties. When he asked why she had ceased to believe, she replied, "I started reading the Bible."

The blogger then began to list some of the "atheist-maker" passages in the Bible that bring some readers up short. These included not just the big-scale horrors—the mass killings, plagues, and wars deliberately wiping out whole nations—but also the soul-cringing rules for dealing with slaves, the stoning of women who committed fornication, the exclusion of physically defective people from tabernacle worship, and the stoning of children who curse their parents.[4]

Blogger David Plotz, who calls himself a lax Jew, decided to give the Bible a serious read. He finished his reading as a "hopeless and angry agnostic." He explained why:

After reading about the genocides, the plagues, the murders, the mass enslavements, the ruthless vengeance for minor sins (or none at all), and all that smiting—every bit of it directly performed, authorized, or approved by God—I can only conclude that the God of the Hebrew Bible, if He existed, was awful, cruel, and capricious. He gives us moments of beauty—such sublime beauty and grace!—but taken as a whole, He is no God I want to obey and no God I can love.[5]

If you think these nonbelievers are overstating their case against God, all they have to do is shove the pages of the Bible itself in your face. Scripture tells us God hardened Pharaoh's heart against his command and then sent an angel of death to kill the firstborn of every family in Egypt. God ordered the armies of Israel to kill and drive out the Canaanite nations, including women and children, from the land they had occupied for generations. He flooded the earth, drowning all life with the exception of the one family he called into Noah's ark, as well as some animals. He devised a detailed and stringent set of laws that were impossible for his people to follow—many of them seemingly trivial and arbitrary as the "atheist-makers" noted above—and warned them that disobedience would bring severe punishment, even execution. These laws included rules for owning slaves and sacrificing innocent animals.

Popular atheist Richard Dawkins famously wrote,

> The God of the Old Testament is arguably the most unpleasant character in all fiction: jealous and proud of it; a petty, unjust, unforgiving control-freak; a

vindictive, bloodthirsty ethnic cleanser; a misogynis-
tic, homophobic, racist, infanticidal, genocidal, fili-
cidal, pestilential, megalomaniacal, sadomasochistic,
capriciously malevolent bully. Those of us schooled
from infancy in his ways can become desensitized to
their horror.[6]

Dawkins is a little more sympathetic to Jesus in the New
Testament,[7] but honestly, it could be argued that Jesus was not
any "better," so to speak. He told his followers that they must
abandon their own families in order to be worthy of him (Luke
14:26). He spoke of his second coming, when he would consign
his enemies to eternal punishment (Matthew 25:31-46). He
consistently taught what is considered by many to be the most
horrifying and offensive doctrine of the Bible—the doctrine of
hell (Matthew 23:33; Mark 9:45; Luke 12:5).

These are some of the most difficult challenges that any reader
of the Bible will ever face. For many (such as those mentioned in
our chapter opening), these challenges to God's goodness come as
a shocking surprise. Others find ways to turn off their consciences
as they make their way through certain stories of the Bible. Some
may be tempted to downplay the severity of these challenges, as
if they can be solved by a couple of snappy answers that would
fit on a bumper sticker. Others might attempt to bury or ignore
them, hoping that by focusing on more uplifting biblical topics
these darker passages will fade into oblivion. When it comes to
difficult questions they can't answer, a lot of Christians hastily
chalk them up to the unfathomable mystery of God. "God works
in mysterious ways," they say, and leave it at that.

Who are we kidding? The concerns skeptics raise about God's
behavior in the Bible are more than valid. They deserve proper

attention and careful study to determine whether the goodness of God can be maintained in the face of these disturbing passages.

The Necessity and Nature of God's Goodness

Despite the contrary claims of atheists and the uncertainty of neophyte Christians, the Bible repeatedly proclaims that God is good.[8] This proclamation is vital because Christianity stands or falls on whether it is true in the most absolute sense. Without the foundation of God's goodness, Christianity collapses into rubble. Who wants to worship a seemingly evil and fickle God? If God is not good, all rationale for moral behavior collapses. As Fyodor Dostoevsky wrote in *The Brothers Karamazov,* "Without God and the future life, everything is permitted."[9]

In spite of the Bible's assertion of God's goodness, it seems, as one pastor put it, there are some "skeletons in God's closet."[10] Big, nasty skeletons just sitting there, rotting in the dark. The smell is impossible to ignore and difficult to bear. We might try to keep the closet door closed, but it just doesn't click shut. It swings right back open. That is why we felt compelled to write this book. We will open wide this closet door and shine a clear and bold light on the putrid carrion behind it.

In the face of these troublesome skeletons, you may assume our defense of God's goodness to be so challenging that we will be forced to indulge in a lot of evasiveness—that in many cases, we will merely show that God's severe acts are not really quite so bad as you might think. No! We assure you emphatically that is not our intention. We have spent years wrestling with these questions, reading material from both sides of these arguments, and engaging in conversations about them from many different perspectives. As a result, we are prepared to stand upon and defend the thesis of this book: *God is good.* When we say good, we really mean *good*. Not just palatable. Not just tolerable. Not just "Okay, I guess I can live with this." We mean that every act God initiates is always right and is designed to produce the best possible outcome in every circumstance. Furthermore, we mean that every act of God in some way expresses his love, patience, benevolence, mercy, and grace. That is the resounding call upon every page of the Bible, both in the Old Testament and the New Testament.

We emphatically reject the premise that God is good *in spite of* the difficult passages of the Bible. Our aim is to show God is good *within* the difficult passages. This means a great deal more than simply explaining the difficulties and then saying, "So you see, it's not as bad as it seems." Suppose I hated the taste of venison, and you told me it was because I had never eaten it cooked properly. So you slaved over a venison dinner for me, and after eating it, I said, "Well, I guess it wasn't as bad as I expected." That response would leave a very different impression than if I said, "Wow! This was really good!"

When we say that God is good, we are saying that when we understand the results of his acts and the motivations behind them, he is shown to be not merely "not as bad as we thought," but absolutely and unwaveringly just, loving, merciful, and morally perfect in all his ways.

Reading the Bible "Properly"

Isaac Asimov was a professor of biochemistry and a prolific twentieth-century author. He was known mostly for his science fiction novels, his seriously impressive sideburns, and his now-famous quote: "Properly read, [the Bible] is the most potent force for atheism ever conceived."[11] This is not the first time we have seen the Bible wielded as a weapon against Christianity.

But we have more often seen people come into Christianity because they dared to brush the dust off that book and open its pages. No doubt Asimov was aware that Bible reading can have that effect as well, so he had to qualify his statement by saying the Bible produces atheists when "properly read."

Properly read? That is a bold statement from someone with no formal theological training. And yet Asimov is just one voice among many in the atheist community claiming to have a better understanding of the Bible than those who have committed their lives to studying its words. How is it that atheists claim to have the high ground here?

The answer is quite simple: Christians yield the high ground because they lack sufficient knowledge to defend it. They lack this knowledge because most Bible teachers never bother to teach all of Scripture; they teach what they like and gloss over what they don't. So when atheists pick up the Bible and discover Moses commanding the Levites to run around with swords and kill their own people,[12] they condemn God for his murderous vindictiveness and assume they are reading the Bible more perceptively than Christians. Then, when these atheists challenge Christians to defend God's outrageous command, the Christians are caught flat-footed without answers; they were never taught to understand the passage. This only serves to affirm the atheists' claim that they are the only ones who maintain the objectivity needed to read the Bible properly. It may be true that many Christians have avoided or glossed over the difficult passages, but it doesn't follow that atheists have filled this void with valid theology.

Properly read, the Bible—every page of it—shows us a God who is exactly the kind of God we need in this broken world. If we are right about this, then we will not need to resort to any mutilation of the Bible or semantic gymnastics to make our point. Playing loose with the text is no help to anyone. Many of the acts of God we address in this book are easily explained and defended on the basis of widely accepted logic and morality. We are, however, going to challenge the way you think about the rationale behind some of God's more puzzling acts.

To read the Bible properly, it is necessary to establish three ground rules that all readers ought to find reasonable given the nature of our subject. If you are an atheist or a skeptic, you may find some of these rules challenging. Many of the Bible's claims are based on beliefs you probably would not accept. Yet at the outset, we must lay before you some of these biblically assumed truths because they provide the underlying rationale for certain acts of God that we are setting out to defend. To put it another way, certain overarching beliefs proclaimed in the Bible provide a logic that sets the foundation for all of God's acts. While you may not share these beliefs, we hope you will be fair enough to take them into account for the sake of argument. So before we proceed further, let's look at these three rules for reading the Bible properly.

The first standard for assessing God's acts and judgments is to recognize that if he does exist, his endgame differs from that of the unbeliever. Given the potential for humans to inherit eternal life—a doctrine asserted throughout the Bible—suffering and death are not the ultimate evils. Indeed, death is the passport from a fallen world of pain and suffering into an unending life of unbounded joy and bliss. The recognition of this fact shines an altogether different light on many passages in which God's judgment seems to inflict death on innocent people. A prime example is God's command for the Israelite armies to march into the settlements of Canaan and drive their swords through the hearts of all the inhabitants, including women and children. This command presents deeper issues that we will address in a subsequent chapter, but it helps to understand that the simple fact of death is not the ultimate evil in God's overarching economy. This recognition that death is not an end but a beginning gives us a vital underlying perspective from which God's judgments can be seen as rational.

Second, to read the Bible properly when probing to find God's goodness in his more puzzling acts, we must have a clear understanding of what goodness really is. Is goodness the same in all circumstances? A chocolate bar is a fine treat for a healthy child but harmful to a diabetic. If we ever hope to discover the goodness of God within the difficult passages of the Bible, we will often need to adjust our understanding of goodness. We will need to see beyond the controversial act we question and uncover the greater but initially opaque good that results from it.

Does adjusting our thinking about goodness mean we will ask you to believe that owning slaves and plundering cities and killing firstborn babies is intrinsically good? No—not at all! But it might behoove us to look beyond these acts—as we will do in subsequent chapters—to see what made them necessary and consider the greater good that came from them.

In our own experience, we witness events that seem tragic, destructive, or counterintuitive but produce good results. Forest fires, for example, are terribly destructive to animals and valuable resources. But fires also keep vital forests from dying by burning away dead and decaying matter, removing deadly plant diseases and harmful insects from the ecosystem, and returning trapped nutrients to the soil.

A story is told of a man who looked out his window one spring day and saw a pair of birds building their nest in a tree across the street. He went out and plucked the nest from the tree and destroyed it. A neighbor woman saw what he did and was shocked at his despicable act. On the following day, the birds began to rebuild their nest in the same tree, and again the man went out and tore it away. The neighbor woman could hardly believe anyone could be so evil. When he destroyed the nest a third time, the livid woman went out and dressed him down in no uncertain terms for his appalling cruelty. The man explained, "Yes, it's a terrible thing to do, and I wish I didn't have to do it. I love birds, and I hate to cause them stress. But you see, I've learned that in two weeks the city will begin widening our street, and all the trees next to the curb are coming down. Only by destroying their nest could I force these poor birds to build elsewhere in time to raise their little ones."

The only way this man could prevent a grim avian tragedy was to commit an act that looked blatantly evil on the surface. It is often that way with God. Sometimes his severity actually gives evidence of his mercy and love.

The third and final rule for reading the Bible properly is to recognize the obvious fact that higher beings can understand lower beings, but not vice-versa. For example, a dog understands very little of what we humans do. To your canine pet, it must seem a silly waste of time for you to sit immobile in a chair with your thumbs punching a little slab of glowing plastic when you could be tossing a frisbee to him in the neighborhood park. Though your dog knows nothing about what makes you tick, you can understand everything necessary for the happiness and well-being of your dog.

If there is a God, we would expect him to understand all the intricacies involved in the complex workings of the universe, whereas such vast knowledge is beyond the reach of human minds. God, therefore, is in a position to understand how an act that seems severe may be the only way a good result can be achieved. God's position as creator enables him to see ultimate good outcomes in advance. As we read in Isaiah 55:9, "For just as the heavens are higher than the earth, so my ways are higher than your ways and my thoughts higher than your thoughts." This passage tells us to expect that some things will never make perfect sense to us. This means there may be times when we must be willing to accept the fact that certain actions will make perfect sense to God but not to us.

This brings up a point we must address. Is there a sure answer for absolutely every challenge to God's goodness? Of course not. Our limited knowledge prevents that. In the cases where we don't have an answer, wisdom dictates we rely on what we do know about God in order to trust him. When we loan a family member $100, do we know for sure they will pay it back? No, but if we've loaned that person money before and it has always been repaid, that knowledge can make us more willing to extend trust. We can do the same when it comes to trusting God. As you will see throughout this book, there is such ample evidence of his goodness—even in the difficult passages of the Bible—that we can trust his goodness even when we find actions we cannot explain.

Don't worry—in this book, we are not going to invoke the high mysteries of God's ways as an escape hatch in those few cases when the rationale for God's actions cannot be determined with certainty. In those instances, we will give you the options we have gleaned from Christendom's best scholars and leave the choice to you.

We can be thankful, however, that God does not require us to believe without evidence and blindly trust that he is good. He has revealed his goodness in the Bible, even in the places where we would least expect to find it. We may not understand everything, but we can understand enough. We don't expect that after reading this book you're going to raise your hands and praise God for killing 3,000 Israelites after they made the golden calf at Sinai. But when you discover the larger context for that severe punishment, you may be willing to accept that something deeper was going on in God's mind that would lead to an ultimate good.

God, Hitchens, and the Wizard of Oz

There is a song in the musical *Wicked* where the Wizard of Oz sings in defense of his questionable practices. He plays loose with words to persuade Elphaba that his deceptive lies toward the people of Oz are justified and even noble. It goes to show that people can spin almost anything in whichever way they want. When I (Matthew) started reading the atheist Christopher Hitchens, I couldn't help but notice he was a master of spin. He used colorful adjectives, adverbs, and prepositional phrases to manipulate the feelings of his readers against God and religion in general. Hitchens's extreme bias against religion led him to force a negative spin on biblical accounts that were actually quite positive. He did this even to the point of calling God's wise commandment to rest once a week "a sharp reminder to keep working and only to relax when the absolutist says so."[13]

The last thing we want to do is commit the same error in the opposite direction. Due to the nature of this book, however, we *will* be looking for every opportunity to observe God's goodness even when a surface-level reading of Scripture appears to cast God negatively. This approach, though technically biased, is biased *because* we are following the obvious intent of the Bible's authors. Don't you find it odd that these authors who wrote about God's actions and judgments in ways that seem negative to us actually believed and taught that God is good, faithful, merciful, and worthy of praise? Why would they so adamantly assert God's goodness while, at the same time, record acts that seem so terrible? Were they just stupid? Barbaric? Primitive?

Let's not assume the worst in people or their beliefs. Let's do the research, climb into their world, and hear them out. Let's actively look into the places where God offends our sense of rightness, morality, and goodness and see if his goodness can truly be maintained. Hitchens put a negative spin on everything religious because that was his agenda as an atheist. We as Christians have an agenda too, but it goes with the grain of the Bible, not against it. If you are genuinely trying to understand what God and the Bible are all about, shouldn't you follow writers who affirm its message rather than disparage it?

God's Open Closet Door

Several months ago, I (Matthew) was invited to lead a Bible study at one of my church's home groups. I was told to choose between one of the two passages listed on that week's Bible reading plan: Joshua 11 or Mark 9. If I chose Joshua 11, we would be looking at a massive battle in which the army of Israel destroyed legions of Canaanite warriors and decapitated a couple of their kings. If I chose to teach from Mark 9, we would be looking at the life and ministry of Jesus. I chose Joshua 11.

On the day I was to teach, one of the leaders turned to me with a quizzical look and asked, "Why did you choose Joshua 11?" I had chosen it for a specific reason, but to be honest, I was now second-guessing myself and asking that same question. It's not as though I am drawn to the violent pages of the Bible. Like most Christians, I naturally gravitate toward the positive stories where love and compassion are readily apparent. Something

G-rated. Joshua 11 does not fit that bill. It is one of the difficult passages of the Bible—difficult because it challenges the belief that God is good.

I chose to teach on Joshua 11 because I knew this difficult passage to be one of the "skeletons in God's closet." Christians don't want to go there in fear of what they might discover, while atheists love to go there to prove that our belief in a good God is indefensible. But for anyone concerned about truth, there is no alternative but to shine a light through that closet doorway and deal honestly with what is there.

When you think about it, doesn't it seem a bit curious that God has left this closet door open? This troublesome stuff is not hidden in a secret compartment of the Bible. It seems obvious that God is unafraid to show us his past. Maybe there is a reason he has left the closet door unlocked. Maybe there are things going on in these difficult passages that we need to understand. Maybe these challenging accounts show the depths of God's goodness in ways that our superficial readings miss. As we end this chapter and begin to peer into God's closet, we make no bones about what we will discover there (pun intended). We will find that once the light of truth hits these skeletons, they will disappear like a mirage. The light will reveal them to have been phantoms without substance—illusions lacking reality, much like the night-time monsters children imagine hiding under their beds.

We pray the in-depth study of these skeletons in the pages that follow will show our skeptic friends that belief in God's absolute goodness is rational and defensible. We hope it will give our fellow Christians more effective ways to defend the truth we often so glibly assert—that God is good. Always good. All the time.

2

Humanity's Rough Beginnings

All religions are cruel, all founded on blood; for all
rest principally on the idea of sacrifice—that is, on the
perpetual [destruction] of humanity to the insatiable
vengeance of divinity. In this bloody mystery man is
always the victim, and the priest—a man also, but a
man privileged by grace—is the divine executioner.[1]

—MIKHAIL BAKUNIN

God's judgment was not feared, but longed for
by those who suffered. It was welcomed,
because it promised the solution to the
longstanding problem of justice.[2]

—JOHN LENNOX

A few years ago, a recently converted Christian woman ran across an internet article that shook her newfound faith to the core. The article claimed that in placing the forbidden tree in the Garden of Eden and commanding Adam and Eve not to eat its fruit, God was setting up the human race for inevitable failure. Having created these humans, God understood their nature inside out. He knew it was inevitable they would disobey his order. To make matters worse, the writer claimed that God used their failure as leverage to make himself a hero to mankind by saving the couple from the consequences of their disobedience. The article put it this way:

> The moment that Adam and Eve ate that fruit, wheels were set in motion that would ultimately result in the doom of mankind. Without some kind of intervention from God we would all be damned. God does promise to intervene, but it's like building a nuclear bomb and setting it to go off in a large city at 12:00. Then, when all of the people of the city come to you for mercy, you disarm it for them. Does that make you a hero for disarming it or a lunatic for building it in the first place? The whole thing was orchestrated to make us feel dependent upon God. That says a lot about God's character.[3]

This unexpected slam against God drained all the joy from this poor woman's faith. But the problem doesn't stop there! It drills even deeper when we consider the apparent harshness of God's judgment against Adam and Eve when they ate the forbidden fruit. Listen to God's own words in Genesis 3:16-17:

> Then he said to the woman,
> "I will sharpen the pain of your pregnancy,
>   and in pain you will give birth.
> And you will desire to control your husband,
>   but he will rule over you."
> And to the man he said,
> "Since you listened to your wife and ate from the tree
>   whose fruit I commanded you not to eat,
> the ground is cursed because of you.
>   All your life you will struggle to scratch a living from
>   it."

Couldn't they just get a time out?

Actually, yes, that happened too. But they never got a time back in. They were banished from God's beautiful garden, never to return (Genesis 3:22-24).

Here we have the first story of God's judgment in the Bible, and it's a doozy. Pain during childbirth? Struggling to make ends meet? And we know many more disasters snowballed from the couple's disobedience—pain, disease, tragedies, brokenness, accidents, and death. Eating a pretty little fruit doesn't seem any worse than a child stealing from a cookie jar. But no parent would punish a child so harshly for such a trivial infraction. Rather than slamming your Bible shut, you might decide to give God a second chance. Maybe he just had a bad day. If you just keep on reading, perhaps you'll encounter the G-rated God you grew up hearing about. But you would be disappointed. Stories of God's judgment continue throughout the entire Bible, and some of the harshest ones show up in humanity's rough beginnings.

What should we think about these difficult stories of God's judgment? Can we really say God is good when we read about him banishing Adam and Eve? Or drowning humanity by flooding the earth? Or raining fire upon the cities of Sodom and Gomorrah? Or killing the firstborn son of every family in Egypt? It's hard to see the least hint of goodness in any of these extremely severe punishments. Our quest in this book is to reveal God to be good in all he does, so let's take a closer look at each of these stories to see what we can uncover.

The Judgment of Adam and Eve

We shouldn't complain that God was unfair in his judgment of our primeval ancestors unless we are willing to be fair in our judgment of him. So let's try to look at this complaint against God's judgment from his point of view.

We'll begin in the first chapter of the Bible, where God explains why he created humans:

> God said, "Let us make human beings in our image,
> to be like us. They will reign over the fish in the sea,
> the birds in the sky, the livestock, all the wild animals
> on the earth, and the small animals that scurry along
> the ground."
>   So God created human beings in his own image.
>   In the image of God he created them;
>   male and female he created them.
> Then God blessed them and said, "Be fruitful and
> multiply. Fill the earth and govern it. Reign over the
> fish in the sea, the birds in the sky, and all the animals
> that scurry along the ground" (Genesis 1:26-28).

In this passage, we're told that God created humans for a specific purpose: to be his deputy rulers of the newly created earth. He created us in his own image so we could be his agents, reflecting his nature and running the earth as his directors and managers. But God had an even greater reason for creating us that rises above these utilitarian purposes. He wanted creatures he could love and who would love him in return. That is why he planted the tree of the knowledge of good and evil in the midst of the garden and told them that to eat of it would bring death. If they loved and trusted God, they would obey his command. If they doubted his love and chose to follow their own desire to test the forbidden fruit, it would show that they loved themselves more than they loved him.

In choosing the forbidden fruit, Adam and Eve rejected God's purpose, rebelled against his authority, and tarnished his image in them. They messed up his perfect world by turning from him and defining for themselves what they considered to be good and evil. This rejection of God's authority for self-chosen autonomy is what the Bible calls *sin*.

Imagine building for yourself the perfect workshop, then developing a machine intended to keep the place organized. What would you do if that machine malfunctioned and destroyed your workshop instead? Chances are you would dispose of it and head back to the drawing board to try again. As the creator, you would have that right. Likewise, God justly could have destroyed his rebellious humans. Not only did Adam and Eve reject the very purpose for which they were created, their rebellion has blighted his perfect world ever since. For God to cast them onto a trash heap like torn clothing or broken cell phones would make perfect sense. But he didn't do that. Why? Because we weren't created just for the purpose of doing something for God. We were created to be with him forever as objects of his love. Out of love, God refrained from executing the judgment we deserved and instead, allowed us to live. He has been in the process of restoring humanity to himself ever since—and at an enormous cost.

The astonishing price God paid to redeem Adam and Eve and their descendants from their sin more than answers the charge of the skeptic in our opening illustration. The skeptic argued that God planted the forbidden tree knowing the couple would eat of it because he wanted to swoop in afterward and save the day, making himself look like a hero. The charge has no substance because God would have no rationale for going through the extremely tortuous suffering and death he endured merely to make himself look like a hero. Why would a being of his stature even care whether little creatures he made thought him a hero? As we can clearly see, the entire story from creation to fall to sacrificial redemption has nothing to do with God's attempt at vanity. It is one of extreme love beyond all comprehension.

The Perfection Factor

Even though God would have been justified in disposing of the rebellious man and woman, we might still think he punished them much too severely. But what if our problem with the intensity of God's judgment is not that he overestimates the severity of our offenses, but that we underestimate the stature of the one we have offended? Our relationship to God is that of creature to creator, which naturally means we are the lower and he is the higher. Think of it as being like that of a subject to his king, a child to her father, a student to her professor, an employee to his CEO, or a soldier to his general. In any of these relationships, when the lower offends the higher, the offense will be considered more severe than if it occurs between equals. A soldier who gets into a scrap with a fellow private may get extra toilets to scrub. If he gets into a scrap with a general, he will likely be court-martialed. Likewise, when we humans offend God, that offense is far more severe than we can possibly realize. It is severe not merely because of the offense itself, but because of our relationship to the one we have offended.

The high majesty of God is expressed in the Bible by the word *holy*. The term is used to signal God's highness, his sacredness, his separateness from all things impure, and his transcendence above everything creaturely. God is holy not in the sense of having a "holier-than-thou" attitude that scorns those beneath his lofty status; he is holy because he is pure in every respect. As Habakkuk wrote of God, "Your eyes are too pure to look on evil; you cannot tolerate wrongdoing" (Habakkuk 1:13 NIV).

Given what we have learned about holiness, it's apparent that God's holiness is a good thing. But when we became imperfect, it put us in a bad spot. Because he is perfect and holy, God can no more tolerate imperfection in his universe than a homeowner can tolerate mice in her pantry. It is not a matter of choice with God. Anything short of holy perfection is not goodness, no matter how near perfect it may be. God's goodness is absolute, which means all the evil that humanity has brought into his creation must be eradicated. We can survive in his universe only if we allow him to bring us back to perfection.

The sooner we recognize the depth of our imperfection in relation to the holiness of God, the better we will understand the severity of his discipline. This principle applies to the judgment of Adam and Eve and to every story of judgment we have yet to cover. It's a truth that was driven home to the prophet Isaiah when he received a magnificent vision of God seated high on a throne surrounded by angelic creatures. A majestic voice thundered, shaking the pillars of the sanctum and filling it with smoke. Utterly overwhelmed, poor Isaiah cried out, "It's all over! I am doomed, for I am a sinful man. I have filthy lips, and I live among a people with filthy lips. Yet I have seen the King, the Lord of Heaven's Armies" (Isaiah 6:5).

Prior to this moment, Isaiah may have thought his sin was not all that bad. But after encountering the holy God he had offended, he realized he didn't even deserve to live.

I (Josh) experienced a moment somewhat similar to Isaiah's. When I was on my journey to Christ, I encountered questions that put me in a state of personal crisis—questions like, How can a holy God allow me, a grievously sinful person, into his presence for eternity?

Only God could have shown me the following two truths (biblically I was ignorant—I had never been to a Bible study). Through my reading of Romans, I saw these truths:

1. That God took care of all my sins through Jesus's life and death.

2. If I were the only person alive, Jesus still would have died just for me. (Wow! That was a humbling thought.)

These two truths broke down my barriers and alleviated my fear of a holy God.

God's Judgment in the Flood of Noah

Let's face it: The story of the flood of Noah is not as child-friendly as teachers make it out to be in children's church. Such early conditioning may lead us to view the flood superficially as an adventure story of a big boat on a sea with a bearded old man and a petting zoo. But in reality, the flood narrative is a story of extreme judgment. It presents what is possibly the highest death count of any event ever recorded. We seldom consider the grimness of the event. Picture Noah and his family huddled together, locked safely in the ark. They soon hear the patter of rain, lightly at first, but rapidly increasing to a deafening roar. Peals of thunder roll across the sky. The boat shudders as the floodwaters rise around it. The family members gape at each other in horror and grief as they hear screams of panic, the wails of terrified children, and the pounding of fists against the hull of the craft. Suddenly the boat lurches as water erupts from deep in the earth. It breaks free of its props and rolls violently with the mounting waves. The screams and pounding turn to splashing and gasping until all the sounds fade out completely.

The flood story naturally raises this question: How in the world is the goodness of God revealed in such a horrific loss of human life?

The narrative begins by calling out how severely corrupt humanity was in Noah's day. This seems to have been initiated when "the sons of God saw that the daughters of man were attractive. And they took as their wives any they chose" (Genesis 6:2 esv). The passage that follows also indicts the Nephilim/giants/"fallen ones"[4] who may have been the offspring of the "sons of God" and the daughters of man. The identity of the "sons of God" and the Nephilim is difficult to nail down, but it's apparent they were instrumental in causing the rapid corruption of humanity.[5] This much is clear from Genesis 6:5: "The Lord observed the extent of human wickedness on the earth, and he saw that everything they thought or imagined was consistently and totally evil."

We have already discussed how the holiness of God and the severity of sin explains why God was completely justified in bringing on the flood. Because people contaminated God's perfect world with their sin, they were not even entitled to the very air they breathe. God justly could have wiped out humanity completely, just as he could have wiped out Adam and Eve. So perhaps the real question we need to ask is, Why did God save Noah and his family?

The surface answer is that Noah was an upright man, the sole exception to an otherwise corrupted humanity. But the reason goes much deeper. God promised Eve that her distant offspring would redeem humanity from sin.[6] Had God destroyed all humanity with the flood, he would have broken his promise. He had to continue a line through which to produce this promised redeemer. Today we understand God's promise was fulfilled through an extraordinary display of self-sacrificial love when Jesus died on the cross. Had God ever wanted to turn back on his promise and save himself the sacrifice of his own Son, the flood would have been a great opportunity. Instead, we see a display of God's faithfulness fueled by his tenacious love.

God was *justified* in destroying humanity. God was *good* in saving Noah's family.

Despite the corruption of humanity in Noah's day, 1 Peter 3:20 and 2 Peter 2:5 reveal that the time spent building the ark was a display of God's patience while Noah warned the world of impending judgment.[7] God could have given Noah a completed ark ready to board. But instead, he set Noah on a process of constructing the massive ship, which took many years of work and drew widespread attention. Think of the hecklers gathered around Noah and his sons, laughing and jeering at this delusional family for building a ship on dry land as he warned them of impending doom.

Despite the evils abounding in Noah's day, God was patient with the sinful people and gave them fair warning. And he is being equally patient in our day. It has been more than 2,000 years since Christ first came to this planet, and we are warned that he will return to render final judgment over the world. His patience has been an enormous blessing to people, but it will not last indefinitely.

Even after reading this defense of the flood, we can understand that you may still find it difficult to deal with the story. It may surprise you to learn this judgment was, in a sense, also difficult for God. Consider what God revealed about his heart to the prophet Ezekiel: "As surely as I live, says the Sovereign LORD, I take no pleasure in the death of wicked people. I only want them to turn from their wicked ways so they can live" (Ezekiel 33:11). Similarly, Lamentations 3:32-33 says, "Though [God] brings grief, he also shows compassion because of the greatness of his unfailing love. For he does not enjoy hurting people or causing them sorrow." We must take these verses with us when we journey to the flood of Noah or any of the difficult stories of judgment in the Bible. Just as a good judge does not relish sending criminals to death row, neither does a holy God relish executing extreme judgment.

When God Rained Fire on Sodom and Gomorrah

In Genesis 18, we read of the violent destruction of the cities Sodom and Gomorrah. The story begins with God revealing to Abraham his intent to destroy the cities because of the extreme wickedness of their inhabitants. Abraham, whose nephew, Lot, lives in Sodom, is concerned that perhaps not everyone is corrupt, and God's wholesale act of destruction might kill the innocent as well as the guilty. He says to God, "Suppose you find fifty righteous people living there in the city—will you still sweep it away and not spare it for their sakes?" (Genesis 18:24). God agrees to save the cities if fifty good people can be found in them. Then, in an exchange we can hardly help but find humorous despite its seriousness, Abraham begins to bargain with God, asking him to spare the cities for the sake of forty-five good people—then for forty, thirty, twenty, and finally, ten. God agrees to save the cities even if only ten good people can be found within them.

Following this exchange, God sends three men—angels, actually—as representatives of himself to visit Sodom. That night, all the men of Sodom mob the house of Lot, where the angels are staying, and try to break down the door in their determination to rape his guests. Needless to say, the sinfulness of that city is confirmed.

Genesis 19:24-25 captures the severity of the two cities' violent destruction: "Then the LORD rained down fire and burning sulfur from the sky on Sodom and Gomorrah. He utterly destroyed them, along with the other cities and villages of the plain, wiping out all the people and every bit of vegetation." It's difficult to imagine the fear and chaos this disaster caused during those final moments.

Where can we possibly find any goodness of God in a story like this?

We find the first example of it in its revelations of his mercy. God would have spared the entire cities for the sake of even ten uncorrupted citizens. At best, there were four: Lot, his wife, and his two daughters. But even these people are depicted as having serious moral issues![8] Yet God took care to remove them in an act described to us in Scripture as his kindness (Genesis 19:19) and his mercy (verse 16).

God's goodness is also revealed by his extreme care in rendering his judgment against the cities. God does not act impulsively; he examines each situation thoroughly. We see this care exhibited in Genesis 18:20-21, where God says, "I have heard a great outcry from Sodom and Gomorrah, because their sin is so flagrant. I am going down to see if their actions are as wicked as I have heard. If not, I want to know." So God sent an investigative team of three angelic representatives who confirmed, beyond all doubt, that the cities were utterly saturated with wickedness.

What's striking about this elaborate investigation is that it wasn't necessary. The Bible makes it clear God's eyes are every-where (Proverbs 15:3), and no creature is hidden from his sight (Hebrews 4:13). So why the needless investigation? It is for us as readers of Scripture. God is making the point that his judgment is never a half-baked decision. It is careful. It is thoughtful. He wants us to understand that he never judges without having all the evidence at hand.

The Plagues of Egypt and the Angel of Death

The plagues of Egypt in Exodus 7–12 might win the Oscar for being the most iconic display of God's power in the Bible. If you grew up in the church, you may remember hearing these stories presented as an epic showdown between the king of Egypt and the king of the universe. In many ways, that perception is correct. But the plague narratives also entail great tragedy. The tenth and final plague is especially difficult to comprehend. In this plague, God's judgment is rendered by sending the angel of death to kill every firstborn son in all the land of Egypt. Imagine the loud and plaintive cries of lament rising throughout all Egypt as every Egyptian father and mother awakened the following morning to find their oldest son dead! Just the thought of what happened is paralyzing. How could a good God possibly inflict such a horrible judgment on an entire nation?

Let's begin our exploration with a bit of background. Prior to this horrific event, Pharaoh (the Egyptian leader) was hold-ing God's people captive as slaves and forcing them to do hard labor. When God sent Moses to demand their freedom, Pharaoh refused. Moses warned the king that God would send terrible plagues upon the people of Egypt until he relented. Sure enough, the plagues came, one after another. As the disasters kept coming, Moses kept returning to warn Pharaoh that continued refusal to obey God would bring another plague. But Pharaoh remained stubborn. By the time God's hand was poised to send the tenth plague, which would kill every firstborn son in Egypt, the king had witnessed the judgment of God descending nine times like clockwork. Once again, Moses forewarned him and his entire court with specific details about the next horrible judgment waiting to descend. Yet once again, Pharaoh would not budge, and God signaled for the angel of death to begin his grim work.

No matter how you look at the tenth plague of Egypt, it is hard to see in it any trace of God's goodness. But before we accuse God of undue cruelty, we must reckon with the fact that he made it glaringly obvious the plagues would continue unless Pharaoh repented and freed the Israelites from the brutality of slavery. Furthermore, it's doubtful Pharaoh and his officials assumed God was bluffing. Not too long before this encounter with divine power, the Egyptians themselves had inflicted the same tragedy upon God's children, murdering hundreds of Israelite babies in a horrific infanticide that continued for months.[9]

As we can see, God's judgment on Pharaoh was severe, but it demonstrated his goodness in two ways: First, it was just, and second, it offered mercy. His judgment was just in that it was necessary to prevent the continuance of the great evils of harsh oppression and death inflicted upon an innocent people. God's judgment offered mercy through his repeated warnings that Pharaoh's obedience would prevent the plagues from being inflicted at all.

The plague stories show that God's judgment does not come without warning. This fact is evident in many biblical stories of judgment such as the expulsion of Adam and Eve,[10] the destruction of Jerusalem,[11] the preaching of Jonah,[12] and especially the plagues of Egypt. God's care to warn of the consequences of sin is another evidence of his mercy and goodness.

The Egyptian plague stories also confront us with another challenge to God's justice. What are we to think about Exodus 9:12, which says that *God* hardened Pharaoh's heart? If that's the case, why would God hold Pharaoh responsible for his resistance? Our answer is this: The Bible doesn't say God hardened Pharaoh's heart until after the account of the sixth plague, which occurs in Exodus 9:8-11. Earlier, in Exodus 8:32, we read that Pharaoh hardened his own heart. So the Bible makes it clear Pharaoh's heart was already hardened against God from the very beginning of the conflict.

It may be that God hardened Pharaoh's heart in the same sense that the sun hardens clay. The sun does not force clay to harden against its will. Clay hardens when exposed to the sun simply because of its innate chemical composition. This illustration demonstrates how God could have hardened Pharaoh's heart without tampering with his free will at all. Like clay exposed to the sun, Pharaoh hardened himself against God because he had the type of proud heart that would automatically solidify when exposed to a superior power.

Although Pharaoh's hard heart was terrible and brought utter devastation upon his nation, God did put the man's stubbornness to good use. It enabled God to display his power to the surrounding nations as a warning of his judgment against sin (Exodus 9:16). And it worked! Forty years later, when Israel was poised to execute God's judgment by waging war against the Canaanites, a local woman named Rahab informed two Israelite spies that the stories of God's power over Egypt had reached them (Joshua 2:1-11). In 1 Samuel 4:8, we learn that many generations later, even the Philistines recalled what God had done through the plagues, and that brought fear to their hearts.

The news got around. God's judgment does not come without warning.

Surprised by Mercy

Considering all the complaints we hear today about God's severity, you may find it surprising that Bible writers often praised him for being so overwhelmingly merciful. For example, Psalm 78:37-38 says, "Their hearts were not loyal to [God]. They did not keep his covenant. Yet he was merciful and forgave their sins and did not destroy them all. Many times he held back his anger and did not unleash his fury!" For some, God's abundant mercy was even a point of frustration. Jonah complained against God for being *too* compassionate (Jonah 3:10–4:2).

Consider the fall of Jerusalem in 2 Kings 25. Everything about it was horrible. The city was surrounded by the armies of Babylon. All the food was gone. The walls were breached. Homes were burned to the ground. The city was plundered. The people were forced into captivity. Most of them would die as prisoners in a foreign land. Here's the kicker: The Old Testament prophets made it clear that these calamities were God's judgment for their rebellion. Decades later, a remnant of the Jews was released to return to their land and rebuild their city. Looking back on the entire ordeal, the prophet Ezra prayed to God, saying, "What has happened to us is a result of our evil deeds and our great guilt, and yet, our God, you have punished us less than our sins deserved and have given us a remnant like this" (Ezra 9:13 NIV).

As we look more closely at God's severe judgments, we can see that the Bible is drenched in his mercy. Swimming in it! Many of us don't see it this way because, deep down, we don't realize the severity of our own offenses against God, and thus we view the sins recorded in the biblical record in a similar light. But if all offenses against God deserve death, as we're assured they do according to Romans 6:23, why should the massive number of deaths recorded in the Old Testament surprise us? Rather, we should be surprised at the number of people who sinned against God, who is holy, and yet were allowed to live! Why else would Paul have to explain in Romans 3:25-26 why God was so *merciful* in Old Testament times?

Welcoming Judgment

In the Nuremburg trials of Nazi officials shortly after WWII, many generals, state officials, and others complicit with Nazi atrocities were condemned and executed for their war crimes. When the gavel went down against them, the world breathed a sigh of relief that judgment had been carried out. This judgment was especially vindicating for the surviving Jews and other people groups who were targeted, captured, beaten, tortured, and gassed to death under the Third Reich. Although their wounds would never fully heal, they finally experienced at least some sense of closure.

There are times when we all want judgment to come down like a hammer on an anvil. When a murder, rape, kidnapping, or other heinous act is committed, we feel a longing for justice arising inside of us. We don't want the authorities to sit and watch passively as evils undermine our society. Deep down, we know judgment is needed to preserve order and is therefore good. God's judgments are rendered for that very purpose. Psalm 9:8 tells us, "He will judge the world with justice and rule the nations with fairness." The challenge we face with God's judgment is not so much that he does it, but that to us it often seems unfair. It seems like *overkill*.

In this chapter, we have tried to show the basic rationale for some of God's early judgments on humanity. We have offered several insights from a biblical perspective to demonstrate that those judgments were necessary not only because they aligned with God's holiness, but also because they are founded on just, rational, moral, and even merciful principles. Even if you are a skeptic who doesn't buy into God's existence, we hope this chapter has helped you see some of his recorded acts and character in a better light.

Even the most devout Christians may squirm at the severity of God's recorded judgments as they fully embrace the goodness of God in everything he does and is. But when you think about it, we should *not* be comfortable with God's severity. We should allow the intensity of the troubling stories to grip us, to make us uneasy. But instead of reacting against God, we should read those stories as Scripture and let them do what they were intended to do, which is to expose our own naïve sense of self-righteousness and bring us trembling to our knees before the God of this universe, who is serious about sin. After all, the judgment of God was not *just* an Old Testament thing.[13] It is a present and coming reality.

3

When "Holy War" Doesn't Sound Holy

The Big Bad Wolf blew down some flimsy
cartoon houses. The God of the Old Testament
destroyed whole civilizations...Can you think
of a fictional villain who was worse?[1]

—DAN BARKER

One big problem for any interpreter is this:
we're dealing with an Old Testament text
that is remote in both time and culture.
In many cases, the New Atheists aren't all that
patient in their attempts to understand
a complex text, historical contexts,
and the broader biblical canon.[2]

—PAUL COPAN

I (Matthew) was caught off guard. As a young junior in college, I
was in charge of a Bible study for a small group in one of our dormitories. Normally our conversations went smoothly, but this time
was different. Our lesson brought us to the era when God commanded the Israelites to go to war against the Canaanite people,
both killing them off and driving the rest from their lands. During

my teaching, I noticed one of the students was becoming visibly distraught, and eventually he spoke up. "Wow…," he said, "this is…very different from the God of peace and love that I grew up learning about." At that moment, all eyes turned on me, the group's young spiritual leader, as if to say, "The guy's got a point. We're waiting to hear your answer." Evidently, this distraught freshman was never exposed to Bible passages about God-sanctioned warfare, and now he was faced with a dilemma: *How could a good God command his own people to commit genocide against other nations?* To be honest, I didn't know what to tell him at the time. (To be brutally honest, I struggled with the passage myself!)

I gave my best shot at some quick pastoral advice before rushing to move on with the lesson. But all of us could tell that the elephant was still tromping around in the living room. The young, troubled student's attendance began to wane, and soon he quit showing up. To this day, I don't know whether this unexpected encounter with the Canaanite wars destroyed his faith.

Stories of God-endorsed warfare in the Bible are not easy pills for Christians to swallow, and God's command for Israel to wipe out the Canaanites might be the hardest to wash down. Outspoken atheists and skeptics take aim at the Canaanite wars as easy targets for shooting down any claim that God is good.

All across history, the screams of Canaanite families are still heard as time after time one nation attempts to annihilate another. We saw it in Hitler's wholesale slaughter of Jews, the Islamic nations' repeated attempts to drive Israel from their land since 1948, the expulsion of Germans from Czechoslovakia, the Soviet Union's deportation of minorities from Crimea, and the more than 500,000 lives lost in the "ethnic cleansing" of Rwanda. These examples are heartbreaking for anyone with a conscience. Yet we must ask: Is there any difference between these terrible atrocities and what God commanded the Israelites to do to the Canaanites?

"Show them no mercy."

God issued his marching orders against the Canaanites through his servant Moses in Deuteronomy 7. Moses was speaking to the people of Israel about their entrance into the land of Canaan. This land was to be their new place of residence after their successful escape from slavery in Egypt. Here is what Moses said:

> When the LORD your God brings you into the land you are about to enter and occupy, he will clear away many nations ahead of you: the Hittites, Girgashites, Amorites, Canaanites, Perizzites, Hivites, and Jebusites. These seven nations are greater and more numerous than you. When the LORD your God hands these nations over to you and you conquer them, you must completely destroy them. Make no treaties with them and show them no mercy (Deuteronomy 7:1-2).

This passage becomes the backdrop for the next book of the Bible, the book of Joshua. After Moses dies, Joshua leads the Israelites into Canaan. True to God's command, the Israelites go to war against the inhabitants. Their first target is Jericho. God told the people of Israel to march around the city for seven days. On the seventh day, they were to march around it seven times, then give a loud shout (some battle plan!). So they shouted, and the walls came tumbling down. Sound familiar? Something you may *not* remember, however, is what immediately followed: "The

Israelites charged straight into the town and captured it. They completely destroyed everything in it with their swords—men and women, young and old, cattle, sheep, goats, and donkeys" (Joshua 6:20-21).

Imagine living in Jericho at the time, going about your day. Suddenly your four walls come crashing down, filling your city with a thick cloud of dust, impairing your vision, and darkening the sky. Moments later, blood-curdling screams split the air all about you. Chaos ensues. What's going on? From the swirling haze emerge silhouettes of men rushing toward you. Their swords flash about them, already dripping the blood of your neighbors.

So Jericho falls by the sword of Israel and their God. One city down. Many more to go.

Next comes the city of Ai. With his confidence bolstered by the victory over Jericho, Joshua sends a small squad to take out their second target. This time, however, they are overcome and chased back to the camp. Confused and frustrated, Joshua asks God why they were defeated. He discovers that Achan, a fellow Israelite, had defied God's orders by hiding stolen treasure from Jericho. Achan and his whole family are sentenced to death, and the armies of Israel march out against Ai a second time. They develop a plan to lure Ai's army away from the city while another Israelite squadron storms in. It works. "So the entire population of Ai, including men and women, was wiped out that day—12,000 in all" (Joshua 8:24-25).

Jericho and Ai get the greatest attention in the Canaanite wars. But reading on, even more bloodbaths take place against the Canaanite kingdoms. Inhabitants are killed. Cities are captured. Heads are lopped off. The conquest of Canaan piles one massacre upon another.

Addressing the Problem

It's not hard to see why even Christians find these conquest stories disquieting. After surveying all the violence and bloodshed, we find ourselves faced with a difficult and disturbing enigma: that the God who calls himself "good" in Scripture would command his people to do something which looks very much like genocide.

As we begin exploring this complicated issue in depth, we must recognize how these stories fit into their historical and theological context. God made a promise to the patriarchs of Israel that he would make their descendants into a great nation and give them the land of Canaan (Genesis 12:7; 26:3-4; 28:13). Would God really come through? Would he fulfill his promise? This is the real tension in Joshua, and the resolution is a resounding yes! In fact, more than one-third of the book is not about the conquest at all, but a description of how the land was divided among the tribes of Israel after the battles were over.[3] All of it points back to a good God who is able and faithful to fulfill his promise.

"Stop right there!" you object. "That doesn't remove the fact that God was willing to fulfill his promise at the expense of others! We can't call God good if his good purposes are accomplished through evil means." True enough. We agree. So how do we make sense of God ordering the Canaanite wars? Old Testament professor Charlie Trimm has observed at least four different proposals that have been offered in response.[4] Let's explore each of them.

Proposal 1: God Is Not Truly Good

One common proposal is to conclude that God must not actually be good. Instead, advocates for this view see him as a tyrant, a bully, and a xenophobic racist. Their own conscience makes it practically impossible for them to worship this God (that is, if he even exists). This is the response you would expect from an outspoken atheist or skeptic. Indeed, many of them consider this to be the *only* appropriate response. If (as they often think) your only two options are to deny the goodness of God or affirm the goodness of genocide, then the answer seems unquestionably obvious.

It's no surprise that we do not endorse this perspective. It's not because of our agenda as Christians to write a book defending the goodness of God. Even if we were to study the Bible's view of God as disinterested non-Christian readers, there is still the fact that the Bible proclaims God is good[5] and unchanging.[6] It would behoove us as seekers of truth to dig a bit deeper into the Bible to find out why it can make this claim of God's goodness in the face of his acts that seem to deny it. To be fair, we would have to conclude either the Bible's definition of goodness is based on deeper principles than we have uncovered, or the Bible is simply inconsistent with itself.

Here, we uncover the key to the problem. Before we can affirm that God is always good, we must understand goodness rightly. We tend to equate good with concepts such as soft, happy, kind, gentle, safe, or pleasing. True goodness goes far beyond these surface concepts. Readers of C.S. Lewis's Narnia books will remember when the beavers explained to the Pevensie children that Aslan, the Christ figure in the stories, is a lion. "Then he isn't safe?" asked Lucy. "Safe?" said Mr. Beaver. "Who said anything about safe? 'Course he isn't safe. But he's good. He's the King, I tell you."[7] As we discussed in the previous chapter, God is a holy God of justice. This is a *good* thing but not a soft thing. It puts those who flout justice in a bad spot, as it did the Canaanites (as we will see later).[8]

Proposal 2: *The Old Testament Does Not Accurately Record God's Dealings with Humanity*

Another way some have argued for the goodness of God in light of the Canaanite wars is by suggesting that the Old Testament (which includes these stories of Joshua's conquest) was written by people who misrepresented God's actions. Advocates for this view maintain that God is good by insisting he never commanded the Canaanite wars or they never even happened, despite what the Bible says. For instance, what if Moses's instructions for the Israelites to invade Canaan, as recorded in Deuteronomy, was only his *perception* of God's orders? What if God intended this false perception of himself to be recorded in Scripture so he could show how much *better* he really was through Jesus? Or, what if the Canaanite wars were only a metaphor for teaching obedience to God? What if these stories are in the Bible as harsh reminders of what happens when we don't show love and compassion to our neighbor? All these ideas have been bounced around.[9]

Although Christians may find these views attractive because they easily solve the dilemma, they present their own problems. It's hard to imagine that God would choose to shape Scripture in the form of historical information if it wasn't actually historical. A plain reading of Joshua and Deuteronomy tells us that God commanded the Israelites to annihilate the Canaanites, and they obeyed. The text itself offers no clues to suggest otherwise, which means any alternative interpretation must be forced into the text.

Despite these problems, many feel that an alternative interpretation that gets God off the genocidal hook is justified because the Bible encourages us to view God through the lens of Jesus Christ. Although it is true that God's revelation in the Old Testament was incomplete[10] and that Jesus is the perfect revelation of God,[11] we cannot go so far as to say that the

Old Testament was *wrong* about God. First, Jesus spoke many harsh words against his Jewish critics, but he never condemned them for taking the Old Testament narratives as actual history. Second, Jesus often assumed God's harsh displays of judgment in the Old Testament to be historical and justified (Matthew 11:23; 24:37-39; Luke 17:29), often warning his audiences that these judgments will happen again (Matthew 11:24; 24:40-41; Luke 17:30). Third, Jesus affirmed Moses and the prophets as authoritative (Matthew 5:17; 7:12; 24:15; Mark 7:9-13; Luke 16:16-17, 31). Fourth, the book of Revelation pictures Jesus rendering violent judgment against the unrighteous (Revelation 2:16; 20:23). If the Bible is right about the goodness of God, we must find our solution to the Canaanite wars somewhere else.

Proposal 3: *The Old Testament Does Not Actually Teach That God Commanded the Israelites to Commit Genocide*

What if, instead of the Bible being wrong, *we* got the Bible wrong? What if the battles in the book of Joshua were not actually what they seem?

Go back to the time of Shakespeare, and you will find a strange world. Reading *Romeo and Juliet*, for example, you may see Romeo's famous monologue of his love for Juliet (Act 2, Scene 2) and think that Juliet is the maid for some other woman represented by the moon. But that's because we don't realize the Roman goddess Diana, associated with the moon, represents chastity. That key bit of mythological knowledge changes our understanding of the monologue. How much more can contextual differences lead us to misunderstand the world of the Bible! The Bible is far older than Shakespeare, written in places, times, cultures, and languages that differ greatly from our own. This does not mean the average reader has no access to the meaning of its pages, but it does mean we must be sensitive to the Bible's world lest we fail to understand what it actually intends to communicate.

Many scholars have pointed out that the common characterization of the Canaanite wars is a prime example of this mistake. Granted, what we are about to reveal does not remove the fact that Israelites killed Canaanites by God's command. But it does reduce the enormity of the outrage modern readers feel when they read these accounts. (We believe the following can be a legitimate reading of the biblical text, but we encourage you to research this yourself. For more information, see *Did God Really Command Genocide?* by Paul Copan [Grand Rapids, MI: Baker, 2014] and "The Jericho and Ai in the Book of Joshua," in *Critical Issues in Early Israelite History* by Richard Huss [Winona Lake, IN: Eisenbrauns, 2008].)

First, when God said he would give Israel the Canaanite "nations" (as most English translations put it), we should recognize that these nations were not like modern countries. Reflecting on the seven people groups mentioned in Deuteronomy 7, Old Testament scholar Peter Craigie says, "These *seven nations* would be relatively small states by modern standards, controlling areas of land usually centered around one or more fortified cities" (emphasis in original).[12]

Second, Israel's primary mode of conquest was not slaughter. According to David Lamb, "While the texts that describe Israel's violent obedience get our attention (Josh 10:40; 11:12), the textual image used far more frequently for the conquest is 'driving out' the people of the land (Ex 23:28-31; 34:11; Num 32:21; 33:52-55; Deut 4:38; 7:1; 9:3-6; 11:23; 18:12; 33:27; Josh 3:10; 14:12; 17:18; 23:5)."[13] In light of this, God's command to "devote to complete destruction" in Deuteronomy 7 is probably a mistranslation. John Walton and Harvey Walton argue that a better definition of God's command would be to remove Canaanite identity from the land.[14]

Third, the number of people in the land of Canaan was reduced before the conquest even began. God said he would drive out many of the people with hornets (Exodus 23:28; Deuteronomy 7:20). Also, it's safe to assume that most noncombatants, such as women and children, would have fled, furthering the idea that the Canaanites were "driven out."[15]

Fourth, the Hebrew word '*ir*, often translated as "city" when referring to Jericho and Ai,[16] can be misleading. The word typically means nothing more than "a permanent settlement, without any reference to its size."[17] The flexibility of the Hebrew word means we shouldn't automatically picture Jericho or Ai as large metropolises. Jericho, for instance, would have to have been small enough for Joshua and his men to march around it seven times and still have enough energy left over to conquer the city in a single day.[18] Richard Hess, through a careful examination of geography, archaeology, ancient writings, and the biblical account, has argued that Jericho and Ai were probably fortresses mostly housing guards and officials.[19] If his analysis is correct, then we have further support that the two great battles in Canaan involved relatively few civilians.

Fifth, the Hebrew word translated "thousand" could also mean a single squad of soldiers, even if the head count of the squad was considerably less than 1,000.[20] This opens the possibility that the reported "thousands" of Israelite and Canaanite warriors may have been much smaller in number. Given ancient correspondence records between comparable cities of the time, Hess suggests that the total number of combatants in Jericho and Ai was probably no more than a few hundred.[21] This could explain why thirty-six out of three "thousand" fallen Israelites were enough to melt their hearts with fear, as reported in Joshua 7:4-5.

Sixth, when Joshua tells us the inhabitants were "completely destroyed" or the Israelites "struck all the land" or "left no survivor," we should recognize that these terms reflect the hyperbolic language of the ancient culture.[22] Just as a sports team might say they "destroyed" or "mopped the floor" with their opponents, so Joshua used conventional warfare rhetoric of his time that should not be taken literally. Consider Joshua 10:20 (ESV): "When Joshua and the sons of Israel had finished striking them with a great blow until they were wiped out, and when the remnant that remained of them had entered into the fortified cities…" The text says that they were "wiped out," yet it still acknowledges a remnant of survivors.[23] So this cannot be deceptive language on Scripture's part. Even many conservative apologists and theologians accept this.[24]

Some of these six points are less watertight than others. But all things considered, the warfare portrayed in these stories is probably less dramatic than a superficial reading might lead us to think. Still, we admit these points do not solve our basic problem. Do the stories still portray God as commanding the Israelites to kill? Yes. Is there still warfare? Yes. Do people still die? Yes. Are there still challenges to the goodness of God? Absolutely. But these points have given us a better perspective as we consider our final proposal.

Proposal 4: God Was Morally Justified in Destroying the Canaanites

Earlier in this chapter, we pointed out that God's purpose for commanding the Israelites to drive out the Canaanites was to fulfill his promise to give Israel a land of their own. But he also had a second purpose: to bring judgment upon the wickedness of the Canaanite people.

We have already argued in chapter 2 that our sin against a holy God rightly invokes his judgment. The Canaanites were a vicious bunch, even by the ancient standards of their day.[25] Their extreme and atrocious actions were not trivial or confined to the privacy of their own homes. They ruined themselves and their families with all kinds of sexual indulgences such as incest, bestiality, and adultery.[26]

Worse yet, these actions were contagious. God wanted the Canaanites removed because he knew their destructive practices would creep into Israelite society.[27] Unfortunately, this turned out to be the case. The Canaanites were never fully driven out, and their sinful culture spread exponentially among the Israelites.[28] These sins included what could easily be considered the worst atrocity of them all: The Canaanites were known to sacrifice their own children by fire.[29] There is evidence these sacrifices were conducted in a horrific manner described by the ancient Greek philosopher Plutarch:

> With full knowledge and understanding they themselves offered up their own children, and those who had no children would buy little ones from poor people and cut their throats as if they were so many lambs or young birds; meanwhile the mother stood by without a tear or moan; but should she utter a single moan or let fall a single tear, she had to forfeit the money, and her child was sacrificed nevertheless; and the whole area before the statue was filled with a loud noise of flutes and drums [lest] the cries of wailing should not reach the ears of the people.[30]

The number of children offered in these sacrifices may have reached into the thousands.[31] If God was truly good, wouldn't we expect that he would deal strongly against such horrifying behavior? We would be upset if he didn't!

Ethnic Cleansing, Pacifism, and Modern "Holy Wars"

We believe the above examination of the Canaanite wars provides sufficient reason to maintain confidence in the goodness of God. But there are several more objections you may still find troubling. Let's look at them.

Some have condemned the Canaanite wars as acts of racism or ethnic cleansing. But the Bible is clear this was not an issue of race or ethnicity at all. The fate of the Canaanites was sealed by their terrible sin, not their race. As Moses said in Deuteronomy 9:4, "After the LORD your God has done this for you, don't say in your hearts, 'The LORD has given us this land because we are such good people!' No, it is because of the wickedness of the other nations that he is pushing them out of your way." God also warned Israel that the fate of the Canaanites would fall on them if they made the same mistake (Leviticus 18:24-28).

The two great battles in the book of Joshua (Jericho and Ai) are coupled with two ironic twists. With Jericho, a Canaanite woman named Rahab honored God, and her family was saved. With Ai, an Israelite man dishonored God and was condemned. These are not insignificant side stories to the conquest. They inform us once again that the issue was not about race. It was all about sin.

What about pacifism? I (Matthew) had a friend who once considered himself a Christian. But he became hostile to the Bible because he believed it's never appropriate to commit violence under any circumstance. My friend loathed the violence he saw in the Canaanite wars and considered himself morally obligated to reject God because of it. Evidently, he believed he had a higher sense of morality than God himself.

The fact that God created human life places him in a unique position of ownership over all life. This gives him the right to choose when and how to take life, whether directly or through human agency. Pacifists who reject God might see death as the ultimate tragedy. God, on the other hand, knows that death is merely the moment of transition when one's spirit detaches from his body and passes into eternity. It is the destiny of all humanity (Hebrews 9:27). Whether one lives on earth ten years or ten decades hardly matters when compared to eternity. God knew the heart of each person killed in the Canaanite wars. The wicked received their deserved judgment, while the innocent—perhaps mostly children—found themselves in a place of eternal bliss.

Another objection is this: If we assume God sanctioned the Canaanite wars, would that legitimize modern-day holy wars and crusades against nonbelieving people groups? Absolutely not. Joshua conquered Canaan in direct response to God's command concerning a specific group of people in a specific time period. Had God never commanded these actions, they would have been totally unjustified. It is hard to imagine that God would issue a similar command to his church today. We live in a specific time where God has called us to peace until he returns to render judgment himself (Romans 12:18-21; 1 Peter 2:20-23).

The misguided "holy wars" recorded in Christian history, such as the medieval Crusades, look nothing like the Canaanite wars of the Old Testament. The Israelites were a runaway group of wandering slaves. They were outnumbered.[32] They were easily scared.[33] Most of their strategies made no sense in military terms.[34] They were not preying on the weak; they *were* the weak. They were not fighting for their God; God was fighting for them.

War was, and continues to be, a sad reality of life. Yet the Bible envisions a time when weapons of warfare will be useful only as material to be hammered into tools for preparing soil and pruning crops (Isaiah 2:4). In other words, God looks forward to a time when war will be eliminated. Done. Never again. This is the heart of God for humanity and a sure part of his ultimate plan for the world yet to be fulfilled.

We actually discover God's perspective on war through the Canaan wars themselves. In Genesis 15:13-16, God told Abraham he would wait 400 years for the sin of the Amorites (that is, inhabitants of Canaan[35]) to accumulate.[36] Had the Canaanites changed their ways during this period of waiting, things could have gone much better for them. God was patient with the Canaanites because he is *good*. He doesn't enjoy judgment any more than we do, but he will not wait around forever while depravity and injustice run amok, spreading their poison on the world like aggressive cancers.[37]

God's Perspective on Prostitutes

The story of Rahab is fascinating. This woman was a resident of Jericho before the Israelites destroyed her city. Although many learn about Jericho without even hearing Rahab's part in the story, the Bible gives more attention to her than to the actual battle![38] Why do you suppose this is?

Before the Israelite army crossed the Jordan River into Canaanite territory, two spies were sent ahead and found a place to stay in Rahab's home. When the ruler of Jericho caught word that there were Israelite spies in their city, Rahab hid them from the ensuing search. She confessed to the spies that the whole city was already aware of the Israelites and the strength of their God. Knowing it was futile to go against the God of heaven and earth, she asked the spies to remember her act of kindness and spare her family when the Israelites attacked the city.

The story is striking because Rahab is specifically identified as a prostitute (Joshua 2:1). Her lifestyle was an obvious example of the depravity of Canaanite culture, which led to their judgment. But the book of Joshua makes it very clear—almost obnoxiously so—that when Jericho was destroyed, Rahab's request was honored. This prostitute and her whole family were saved (Joshua 6:22-25).

Rahab's narrative is no side story. In fact, hers is the first story recorded after Joshua assumed command of his army, before any of the battles take place. Why does the book of Joshua lead with her? Because her story helps us understand the Canaanite wars as a whole: that although the warfare was full of violent judgment, the Canaanites knew God was coming, and they knew no one could stand against God. Yet as Rahab's account shows, anyone—even a *prostitute*—could be saved by seeking mercy. Tragically, the rest of the Canaanites did not opt for Rahab's approach. Rather than repenting of their ways in the face of judgment, they stubbornly chose to fight what they should have known to be an impossible battle. As you can see, condemning God for the destruction of the Canaanites is blaming the wrong party. The Canaanites brought about their own destruction.

Rahab shows up in the genealogy of Christ[39] and is praised in the New Testament as a woman of remarkable faith and a model for salvation.[40] It is no wonder that a good God would preface his judgment against Canaan with such an extraordinary story of his mercy on full display.

4

The Bible's Immoral Heroes

To be fair, much of the Bible is not systematically
evil but just plain weird, as you would expect of a
chaotically cobbled together anthology of disjointed
documents...but unfortunately it is this same weird
volume that religious zealots hold up to as the inerrant
source of our morals and rules for living.[1]

—RICHARD DAWKINS

The "historical books" of the Bible are not merely
history books. They are theological works of art that
display God to us and show how to live in response.[2]

—J. KENT EDWARDS

I (Josh) love a good superhero movie. Years ago, when my son was
in grade school, I took him to see one of the Superman movies.
Afterward, we went to a local diner for dessert. For more than an
hour, we discussed all the similarities between Superman and Jesus
we could imagine. What a great teaching tool that turned out to be!
Here are just a few of the similarities I remember:

1. Both Jesus and Superman came to Earth from
    somewhere else.

2. Both had a dual identity. (Superman was the reporter Clark Kent and a superhero. Jesus was a fully human Jewish man and God incarnate.)

3. Both dealt with large-scale events that a normal person could not handle.

4. Both sacrificed themselves in tremendous ways.

5. Both thought of others before themselves.

6. Both wanted to establish righteousness.

7. Both were on a mission.

The list could go on. There was value in using a popular hero like Superman to teach my son about Jesus. The positive qualities of goodness tend to implant more readily when young people see them displayed in the lives of heroes they admire. I wanted to instill Christlike qualities into my son, and it helped show him that his own heroes were emulating qualities that matched the character of Christ.

The Bible contains a lineup of heroic figures of its own—people who get a lot of screen time in Scripture because God used them in powerful ways. But if we were to try to emulate some of their actions or characteristics, we would quickly end up in prison. For example, we read in Exodus 2:12 that Moses covertly killed an Egyptian and tried to hide the crime, yet God still used him to establish his law for the nation of Israel. David, the man God chose to rule Israel and establish a dynasty of kings because "the LORD looks at the heart" (1 Samuel 16:7), also had his hand in murder. To make matters worse, he committed the deed to cover up the fact that he had impregnated his victim's wife (2 Samuel 11). And that was not David's only failing. God allowed him to remain in power despite the fact he was remarkably uninvolved as a father. One of his sons raped one of his daughters and was murdered by another son who later tried to take David off his throne (2 Samuel 13–15). You'd think one of David's eight wives[3] would have talked some sense into him!

And then there is Jacob, the conniving second son who stole the birthright from his older brother and manipulated the breeding of his father-in-law's cattle to increase his own herd. Of all the men God could have chosen, he picked this one to be the patriarch of the twelve tribes of Israel and to give that nation his name.

What does all this say about God's vetting process? How could God align himself with such bad people? Why would he give them a platform of leadership? In Hebrews 11, the Bible's Hall of Fame, Moses, David, Jacob, and other troubled individuals are commended as people of faith. Verse 16 tells us that "God is not ashamed to be called their God." As we can see, the Bible not only gives us troubling examples of moral integrity, but it also raises questions about the God who chose them for great tasks, associated with them, and gave them so much airtime in Scripture. Today the cancel-culture mob would come down hard on these heroes of the Bible, toppling their statues and suspending their Twitter accounts.

Hanging Out with the Wrong Crowd?

In order to understand why God used murderers, liars, cheaters, and frauds, we must step outside our own culture and enter one that is largely alien to us. We live in a time when people denounce association with those who experience moral failure. The rationale is that by associating with these people, we send a message that we endorse their behavior. For us, sometimes this withdrawal of association may be necessary. But for God, that is not always the case. As we will see, this is good news for us.

In Mark 2:15, we see Jesus reclined at a table as he eats with many individuals who are immoral and despised by society's good, upstanding citizens. Commentator James Brooks points out that "in [Jesus's] society table fellowship was one of the most intimate expressions of friendship."[4] This explains why the religious teachers of the law were deeply offended. "Why does he eat with such people?" they asked.[5] Jesus responded to them in Mark 2:17: "Healthy people don't need a doctor—sick people do. I have come to call not those who think they are righteous, but those who know they are sinners."

God associates with sinners! He doesn't do this despite their sin, but because of their sin. Jesus treats them as friends because his method of healing is profoundly relational. He is not afraid of how his associations might tarnish his reputation. He knows they cannot tarnish his character. If we criticize God for befriending people like Moses, Jacob, or David, then we miss the whole point of God's lavish grace, and we stand removed from the dinner table next to those offended religious teachers. Like them, we are blinded by our own moral "piety."

The Heart Beneath the Sin

The sins of Moses, David, and other Bible characters will not be defended in this book. Neither did Jesus defend the immorality of those he dined with. Many who encounter the Bible think the purpose of its stories is to provide textbook examples of moral living by faithful people whose lives we should emulate. This is *mostly* false, yet many church sermons mistakenly use the Bible in this way as if it's mostly true. We're told, "We need to be more like Abraham, more like Moses, more like David, more like Solomon!" These kinds of sermons should be handled with care, lest we back ourselves into a corner whenever our "moral heroes" display their faults.

This isn't to say that there aren't any moral takeaways we can learn from individuals like these. Our point is that these stories are first and foremost about God. God is the one who saves the day. God is the one who never fails. God is the one who shows kindness to those who don't deserve it—people like you and me.

We shouldn't determine morality on the basis of studying flawed people in the Bible. Instead, we should look to the explicit moral commandments of Scripture. When biblical characters like David are seen following those guidelines, we can commend them and use them as examples as long as we keep God as the superhero. But when we read about people trying to honor God and falling flat on their face, we can relate to their struggles and thank God that he shows mercy—not according to the intensity of our sorrow, but according to his steadfast love (see Psalm 51:1).

As we look deeper into Scripture, we can begin to understand more about why God chooses certain men for great deeds despite their flawed lives. We read in 1 Samuel 16:7 that "the LORD doesn't see things the way you see them. People judge by outward appearance, but the LORD looks at the heart." God saw something in the heart of David that was not visible to human perception. On that basis, he chose David to be the king of Israel who would establish a dynasty that would bring Christ himself into the world.

As we have already noted, David sinned grievously, committing adultery with the wife of Uriah, one of his most loyal soldiers. When it became apparent the woman was pregnant,

David had Uriah deviously killed, which enabled David to marry Uriah's widow to cover up his sin. It is natural for us to think that in response, God would at least remove David from his throne, if not slay him outright for stacking up such a pile of horrible sins. But God did not do that. He not only allowed David to live, he also allowed him to remain on Israel's throne.

Wouldn't this lead us to think that God had endorsed what David had done? That he overlooked his sin as unimportant when compared with David's strengths? What do we make of this?

We find the answer when we discover what it means for God to "look upon the heart" of those he chooses for special purposes. This doesn't mean he chooses only those who have a *perfect* heart. Such a heart does not exist in any human in this fallen world. It means a man like David had a heart set on God. He was determined to love God and follow him. But like all fallen humans, his heart sometimes faltered, and he failed to live up to God's standard of goodness, which he dearly desired to follow.

We see David's eagerness to follow God revealed in 2 Samuel 12, when Nathan the prophet confronted David and called out his adulterous and murderous sins. David didn't get defensive. He didn't make excuses. He immediately owned his sins and sought God to forgive him. This was the kind of man God was looking for to be king—not a man of moral perfection, but a man who set God's standard of behavior as his goal. And when he failed, he displayed enough backbone to confess his sin and seek forgiveness.

If any thought lingers that God might have gone too easy on David or that God's continued acceptance of David implied he had turned a blind eye to his sin, reading about the punishments

God imposed for David's sin should remove all doubt. As Nathan the prophet told David:

> From this time on, your family will live by the sword because you have despised me by taking Uriah's wife to be your own. This is what the LORD says: Because of what you have done, I will cause your own household to rebel against you. I will give your wives to another man before your very eyes, and he will go to bed with them in public view. You did it secretly, but I will make this happen to you openly in the sight of all Israel…the LORD has forgiven you, and you won't die for this sin. Nevertheless, because you have shown utter contempt for the word of the LORD by doing this, your child will die (2 Samuel 12:10-14).

God accepted and spared David despite his grievous failures because his deep love reaches out and embraces those who love him and repent of their sins. It is clear, however, that in accepting David and his contrite heart of repentance, God did not for one millisecond condone or accept his sin.

God's Deliverance Through Samson's Stupidity

In Judges 13, we're told about an angel who visited a woman struggling with infertility. The angel promised that she would have a child who would grow up to save her people from the oppression of the Philistines. We read in verses 24-25, "When her son was born, she named him Samson. And the LORD blessed him as he grew up. And the Spirit of the LORD began to stir him." Reading this, we are naturally inclined to think Samson is bound to grow up to be a decent guy, a man of God with exemplary character. Another hero we can emulate.

But no. The first thing we learn about Samson as an adult is his lustful infatuation with a Philistine woman. He demands that his parents get this woman for him so that he might marry her in total disregard for God's command for the Israelites not to intermarry with the Canaanite tribes.[6] Samson's demand is rightly understood as a moral flaw and a breaking of God's law, but Judges 14:4 points out that God is actually at work in Samson's folly, orchestrating a way for Samson to get close to the Philistines.

As the story continues, Samson experiences episodes during which the Spirit of God empowers him with supernatural strength. At the same time, he periodically displays immature rage against the Philistines, which spurs him to slay them in great numbers and destroy their property. A prostitute who is essentially an agent for the Philistine leaders eventually seduces Samson. Then through a record-breaking display of stupidity, he winds up betrayed, captured, and blinded by his enemies. They bring Samson into the temple of their god, where they force him to entertain them like a circus freak.

The temple is a huge building filled with thousands of Philistines, including their rulers. Blind and humiliated, Samson makes one final prayer. No, it's not a sorrowful confession to God. It's not a rededication to a higher moral standard. He prays to God solely for the ability to avenge himself (Judges 16:28). Yet God grants his less-than-morally-impressive prayer request. Samson stretches out his arms against two pillars and, with a mighty effort, breaks them apart, collapsing the building upon multitudes of Philistines and himself as well. His prayer for revenge became God's answer to the oppression of Israel. After forty years of patience,[7] God finally renders judgment against the Philistines through the immaturity of Samson.

Samson's moral character is so checkered that theologian Preston Sprinkle calls him "a self-centered, vengeful porn star enslaved to lust and bloodshed."[8] Yet through all his lust, debauchery, and folly, God's Spirit cooperated with Samson, enabling him to accomplish remarkable things. The literary dance between God's empowering presence and Samson's sin is not only visible; it's in your face! The story intentionally vise-grips these two seemingly opposites together. Clearly, the author is not unaware of this tension; he's drawing you into it. This "hero" of the Bible is frustratingly unheroic, yet God still manages to draw a straight line with a crooked stick. Through Samson, God makes a point about himself, about his providence, and about his ability to work through bad intentions for his good purposes. This echoes the lesson of Genesis 50:20—what people intend for evil, God is able to use for good! But more to the point of this chapter, God's association with morally challenged characters like Samson was never meant to be taken as an endorsement of such people. It was a spotlight on their God, whose goodness trumps human failure.

So how are we to read the scriptural stories in which God accomplishes his purposes through flawed human characters? We do this by admiring the goodness of God, who lavished extraordinary patience and grace over their lives. God is the only *true* hero of Scripture. He possesses the power and perfect moral integrity needed to accomplish all his purposes, yet he chooses to befriend sinful people and use them to play crucial roles in his drama of redemption. Like the characters we are studying in this chapter, not one of us is perfect. In fact, many of us have deep regrets about our past or present failures and feel as though God could never use us. But if God could use someone like Samson, then certainly God can use us.

Jephthah's Ludicrous Vow

As we have seen, many stories in the Bible simply describe the immoral actions of people without implying we should live like them. But one story in particular can be read in a way that actually seems to praise a very immoral action. In Judges 11, we find God partnering with another flawed character in the story of Jephthah (commonly pronounced jep-thaw). According to verses 30-31, the warrior Jephthah made a vow to God, saying, "If you give me victory over the Ammonites, I will give to the LORD whatever comes out of my house to meet me when I return in triumph. I will sacrifice it as a burnt offering." Earlier, we credited Samson with record-breaking stupidity, but Jephthah comes close to stealing that prize from him. What did he expect might come from his house to meet him? A goat with a confetti popper?

Well, God gave Jephthah his victory. Upon his arrival back home, who but his daughter came out to meet him, dancing in joy with a tambourine. Jephthah's response is chilling. Judges 11:35 says, "When he saw her, he tore his clothes in anguish. 'Oh, my daughter!' he cried out. 'You have completely destroyed me! You've brought disaster on me! For I have made a vow to the LORD, and I cannot take it back.'" True to his word, Jephthah sacrificed his own daughter.

Should we honor Jephthah for this strong commitment to fulfilling his promise? Should we commend him for inflexibly performing his duty before the Lord?

If we are not careful with this text, we might come to think that the Bible is actually endorsing Jephthah's pious commitment to his vow. But just because an event is recorded in Scripture does not mean God endorses it. Often, the Bible simply relays information about what happened, leaving us to consider the ethical implications for ourselves. Jephthah's story is meant to take us *deeper*. We reflect on his story by asking, Is it really a greater sin to break a vow than to sacrifice your own daughter? In the Old Testament, God's law included provisions for when people made rash vows that would not be appropriate to keep.[9] Jephthah's understanding of God smells like the religion of his pagan neighbors, not the true manner of worship prescribed to the Israelite people.[10] This becomes all too obvious when we consider the theology of Judges as a whole: Bad things happen when you mix God with false religion.

Some Bible interpreters consider it unlikely that Jephthah actually put his daughter to death, as he would have done if an animal met him on his return from victory. Instead, they think Jephthah bound his daughter to lifelong virginity as a figurative sacrifice. But whether Jephthah's sacrifice of his daughter meant her death or her lifelong celibacy, it does not change the essential immorality of Jephthah's rash vow and his determination to keep it at his daughter's expense. The incident reminds us yet again that God can find a place for even the most flawed individuals to accomplish his purposes. That should be of great comfort to us.

The Problem of Polygamy

Polygamy was considered normal in the culture of Bible times. Jacob, who fathered the nation of Israel, did so through four women—two wives and two concubines.[11] Abraham's wife, Sarah, shared her husband with her handmaiden, Hagar, who thus became the mother of Ishmael, ancestor of the Arabian races (Genesis 16:3-4). We could also point to Lamech (4:19), Esau (26:34), Ashur (1 Chronicles 4:5), Gideon (Judges 8:30), and others.

Were you surprised earlier in this chapter when we mentioned that King David had eight wives? His son and successor,

Solomon, had 700 wives (1 Kings 11:3). Solomon splurged big time! He also had 300 concubines, which were basically servant or slave women kept for the purpose of sexual pleasure and bearing children. With all these wives and concubines, Solomon could have sexual relations with a different woman every week for more than 19 years.

Many in our modern world (and especially Christians) do not believe polygamy is right or good for society. But God obviously chose to associate with polygamous men in order to accomplish his purposes. Does this mean he approves of polygamy? As we have already seen through our studies of David, Samson, and Jephthah, *descriptive* is not the same as *prescriptive*. Just because the Bible *describes* something does not mean it *prescribes* it. God's model for marriage never included multiple wives or husbands (Genesis 2:24; 1 Corinthians 7:2; 1 Timothy 3:2). In fact, the passage in 1 Kings 11, which speaks of Solomon's many wives, explicitly recounts Solomon's rebellion against God.[12] Deuteronomy 17 prohibits kings like Solomon from having multiple wives (and collecting excessive amounts of gold and acquiring horses from Egypt. Solomon did all these things).

Yet didn't God claim to *give* King David his multiple wives? God said in 2 Samuel 12:8, "I gave you your master's [King Saul's] house and his wives and the kingdoms of Israel and Judah." Here, God is reminding David of how gracious he was in giving David the throne of his predecessor. Included in this transfer of power were the former wives of King Saul. In that culture, a king's wives were symbols of prestige.[13] Hence, God gave David all of Saul's prestige as king. That is the point of his statement. Think of a Christian father whose brilliant son has just been accepted into the only university that can offer him the education he needs to succeed in his chosen field. The father knows his son will be required to attend certain classes that teach unchristian values. But the father pays the tuition anyway, hoping he has instilled into his son the integrity and courage to resist the negative influences that will be thrust upon him. Or think of Jesus directing Jewish citizens to pay Roman taxes even though he knew the government supported immorality and oppression (Matthew 22:21). In a fallen culture, it is often best to work within the system even though we do not endorse the corruption within it. Similarly, God did not endorse polygamy by giving David the fullness of Saul's kingly power and prestige. Rather, he was working according to this world's corrupted standard so that David would be fully recognized as the new king of Israel.[14]

Cursing Your Enemies Through Prayer?

Perhaps the most challenging aspect of these various biblical "heroes" is not what they did, but what they prayed. Consider this prayer from David in Psalm 109:6-10 (ESV):

> Appoint a wicked man against him;
>   let an accuser stand at his right hand.
> When he is tried, let him come forth guilty;
>   let his prayer be counted as sin!
> May his days be few;
>   may another take his office!
> May his children be fatherless
>   and his wife a widow!
> May his children wander about and beg,
>   seeking food far from the ruins they inhabit!

On and on David goes, speaking curses upon his enemies. This psalm is considered to be an imprecatory psalm, or a cursing psalm, which is a psalm speaking ill of others. More than a dozen psalms could be labeled imprecatory, at least partially.[15] Reading psalms such as these, we may be tempted to invoke our previous principle of interpretation: Just because the Bible records something does not mean God endorses it. But in this case, it's not that simple. The book of Psalms is a collection of songs and prayers written by David, Solomon, and others, intended to be used for prayer and worship in the life of God's people. If Christians are supposed to pray the psalms, does that really mean we are to follow after David and others who cursed their enemies?

Truth be told, the imprecatory psalms are not the only psalms that may bother the Christian. Many of the lament psalms accuse God of abandoning his people or being indifferent to evil (for example, Psalms 10:1; 22:1; 42:9; 44:24; 74:1-11). Are these psalms models for us to follow? In a word, yes. The writers were modeling *honesty*. They were open. They were raw. They were showing what real relationship is like. The psalms give us permission to pray our feelings honestly before God. This is a good thing! We don't need to polish our prayers and clean ourselves up before we approach God. He can handle our fears, our worries, our doubts, and even our anger.

The Bible teaches that we should not foster hate in our heart against others. Instead, we should love our enemies (Leviticus 19:17; Proverbs 25:21; Matthew 5:43-48). But if we do feel hatred or rage toward our neighbor, we should at least be honest to God about it. The imprecatory psalms give us permission to use prayer as an outlet for such honesty.

Many of these prayers against other people are nothing more than a cry for God's judgment against evil, a subject we already discussed in chapter 2. Psalm 79 is a good example of this. The author, Asaph, recounts all the horrible things the nations have done against God and his people. So he prays in verse 6, "Pour out your wrath on the nations that refuse to acknowledge you—on kingdoms that do not call upon your name." Rather than taking matters into his own hands, Asaph gives them up to God's perfect justice. When we find ourselves wanting to harm others in revenge, we would do well to pray in a similar fashion. Such prayers can free us to follow the wisdom of Paul, who wrote,

> Beloved, never avenge yourselves, but leave it to the wrath of God, for it is written, "Vengeance is mine, I will repay, says the LORD." To the contrary, "if your enemy is hungry, feed him; if he is thirsty, give him something to drink; for by so doing you will heap burning coals on his head." Do not be overcome by evil, but overcome evil with good (Romans 12:19-21).

Looking Back

A good God has good reasons for filling his stories with morally flawed people. Through their failures, his grace is on full display.

Looking back, we see that the Bible is astoundingly honest. It doesn't skirt over the moral flaws of people. It reports both triumph and defeat, progress and setback. It doesn't paint the perfect picture that we might hope to see; rather, it paints a picture that makes sense only when we consider God as the true superhero in a massive movement of redemption from the first to the last chapters of the Bible. If we miss this, we miss everything.

Looking back, we see the Bible is astoundingly realistic. Whereas many religious books like to portray their figures as morally superior people, we know in life that every person is deeply flawed. None of us is perfect. If all the "heroes" of the

Bible were polished, proper, and flawless, we would have stories that might be interesting to read but difficult to relate to.

Looking back, we see that these stories of Bible characters give us more than meets the eye. They show change is needed. Something needs to stop the cycle of sin. Take Samson, for example. The Bible ends his story by pointing out that he killed more at the time of his death than during his life (Judges 16:30). After Samson was betrayed, beaten, and publicly humiliated before the jeering Philistines, he stretched out his arms against those two pillars and saved God's people. But Samson's act of salvation was only temporary. To offer God's people permanent salvation required the heroism of another man—one who was betrayed, beaten, and publicly humiliated before the jeering Jews and Romans. A man who stretched out his arms to die for the salvation of God's people. Only this time, it was a man without Samson's moral flaws. A man who would *save* more people in his death than in his life on earth. A man who is the world's only true superhero.

5

The Traumatic Tests of Abraham and Job

It isn't just that I don't believe in God and, naturally,
hope that I'm right in my belief.
It's that I hope there is no God!
I don't want there to be a God;
I don't want the universe to be like that.[1]

—THOMAS NAGEL

With Paul, I desire to say at the end of my life, "I have
fought the good fight, I have finished the race, I have
kept the faith" (2 Tim. 4:7). And I can't wait to hear
Him say on that day, "Well done, my good and faithful
servant...Let's celebrate together!" (Matt. 25:21, NLT). I
am driven and carried and captured by love. Are you?[2]

—MICHAEL BROWN

We have a mutual friend whose son-in-law qualified for training as an air traffic controller. Despite the fine opportunity,
the decision to join the training program was not easy. He would be
required to quit his job in Dallas and move his wife and two-year-
old daughter to Oklahoma City. There, they would live entirely at
FAA expense for nine months of training, which was known to be

intense and grueling. The students would be tested each month, and only those who passed these tests would be allowed to continue. One failure would send this student and his family packing for home without income and without a job. So you can imagine the heart-pounding pressure that weighs on the students who have to pass that final test!

After wrestling over the pros and cons of the decision, he took the plunge, graduated, and was assigned as an air traffic controller at Dallas-Fort Worth International Airport.

As trying as this young man's tests were, they were like a first-grade math game illustrated with bright colors and dancing fish compared to the tests endured by the two Bible characters we will consider in this chapter. You may have heard of the "Test of Abraham" recorded in Genesis 22—a test in which God asked Abraham to do the unthinkable to his son. You are likely familiar with Job, whose sanity was tested to the limit when God set him on a brutal experience of loss and suffering—something many of us can readily relate to. The traumatic tests experienced by Abraham and Job have placed God, the test administrator, in a harsh light. But as we will see, he had good reasons for placing these two in a pressure cooker.

The Test of Abraham

As you read Abraham's story, try to put yourself in his shoes—especially if you are a parent.

> Some time later, God tested Abraham's faith. "Abraham!" God called. "Yes," he replied. "Here I am." "Take your son, your only son—yes, Isaac, whom you love so much—and go to the land of Moriah. Go and sacrifice him as a burnt offering on one of the mountains, which I will show you" (Genesis 22:1-2).

In this passage, God calls Abraham—this man he has selected to father his chosen nation—to do the unthinkable: to sacrifice his beloved son, Isaac. We readers are told at the beginning that this is only a test. But Abraham did not know that. All he heard was the command from heaven to sacrifice his only son. The story continues:

> The next morning Abraham got up early. He saddled his donkey and took two of his servants with him, along with his son, Isaac. Then he chopped wood for a fire for a burnt offering and set out for the place God had told him about. On the third day of their journey, Abraham looked up and saw the place in the distance. "Stay here with the donkey," Abraham told the servants. "The boy and I will travel a little farther. We will worship there, and then we will come right back."
>
> So Abraham placed the wood for the burnt offering on Isaac's shoulders, while he himself carried the fire [i.e., fire starter] and the knife. As the two of them walked on together, Isaac turned to Abraham and said, "Father?"
>
> "Yes, my son?" Abraham replied.
>
> "We have the fire and the wood," the boy said, "but where is the sheep for the burnt offering?"
>
> "God will provide a sheep for the burnt offering, my son," Abraham answered. And they both walked on together (verses 3-8).

Abraham spent much of his life as a nomad traveling hundreds of miles. But no journey could have felt longer than his march to Moriah with Isaac. When they finally arrived at the mountain, Abraham built his altar, arranged the wood, tied up his son, Isaac, and raised the knife to kill him. Suddenly, an angel from God swooped down and stopped Abraham, saying, "Do not hurt him in any way, for now I know that you truly fear God. You have not withheld from me even your son, your only son" (verse 12). Then Abraham spotted a ram with its horns caught in a thicket. He sacrificed the ram instead of Isaac.

Although the test of Abraham ended with no harm to Isaac, we cannot help but wonder: Why would God put Abraham through such an excruciating trial?

Back in 2014, the Christian community was stirred up by a viral blog post with this provocative title: "I would fail Abraham's test (and I bet you would too)." The author was Rachel Held Evans, an Episcopalian who challenged the status quo of the evangelical church. "I'd like to think that even if those demands thundered from the heavens in a voice that sounded like God's," she said, "I'd have sooner been struck dead than obeyed them… And I'm beginning to think that maybe that's okay."[3]

Evans came under a great deal of heat for her view of the test of Abraham. As we have already seen, Abraham's actions were commended by the angel. They were commended again in Hebrews 11:17. Evans was mistaken, but her blog post forced evangelicals to wrestle with the difficulty of this narrative. We cannot pretend the test of Abraham is a simple story with simple answers. It is extremely unsettling. The fact that the angel stopped Abraham's hand at the last second does not nullify the question: How could a good God ever put a father through such a horrifying ordeal? That God would have Abraham saddle his donkey, chop the wood, ride out, climb the mountain, bind his son, and raise the knife in his hand…*all for the sake of a test?*

I (Josh) didn't grasp the weight of God's request of Abraham until I was giving a parenting talk to an audience where my son, Sean, happened to be present. Partway through my talk, I stopped suddenly as a deep emotion swept over me when I caught a glimpse of Sean. I don't think I could sacrifice my son or any one of my three precious daughters. I just stood there, sober and silent, for several moments. (It was then that I got a small glimpse of what it meant to the Father to send his only Son to the cross to die for me.)

Examining the Exam

Genesis 22:2 shows that God fully understood the weight of his request of Abraham: "Take your son, your only son—yes, Isaac, whom you love so much—and go to the land of Moriah." These tender words reflect God's sensitivity to the moment. But one of the words was lost in translation—the Hebrew word *nā'*. This little word functions to soften the request, similar to how we might say "please" before making a request. According to commentator Victor Hamilton, "*Nā'*, which occurs more than sixty times in Genesis, is used only five times in the entire [Old Testament] when God speaks to a person. Each time God asks the individual to do something staggering, something that defies rational explanation or understanding. Here then is an inkling at least that God is fully aware of the magnitude of his test for Abraham."[4] The tenderness expressed in God's request shows he is not a cosmic bully trying to assure himself that Abraham would mindlessly obey him. Cosmic bullies don't talk like that.

Many casual readers think God was testing Abraham's obedience. But as the NLT rendering of Genesis 22:1 suggests, God set out to test Abraham's *faith*. Obedience, quite simply, is doing what God tells you to do. Faith, on the other hand, is a forward-looking trust in God's promises, *displayed* by a posture of obedience. Every example of faith listed in Hebrews 11 fits this definition. Abraham found his place on that list of faithful individuals specifically for passing the test relating to his son Isaac.[5]

If God was testing Abraham's faith, and if faith is trusting God's promises, what promise of God was Abraham trusting to be true? Our passage does not explicitly say, but it sits within a larger context in which the theme of Abraham's faith is vividly apparent. His story begins in Genesis 12, when God calls him to leave his homeland and set out for a land of promise. "I will make you into a great nation. I will bless you and make you famous, and you will be a blessing to others" (Genesis 12:2). Then, in Genesis 15:4-5, God tells Abraham that his descendants will come from a son—not through many sons, but though one son. At the time, Abraham didn't have any sons, but the next verse says Abraham believed God. He believed God's promise to give him a son who would father a great nation. That's faith (cf. Roman 4).

Yet Abraham and his wife grew old, and the prospect of having children diminished with every passing year. Then in Genesis 18:10, long after Abraham and his wife, Sarah, were of child-bearing age, God says this son will be born before the same time next year. So Isaac is born in their old age, the miracle baby whose presence would remind Abraham every day that God was faithful to keep his promise.

All of this leads up to a climactic moment in Abraham's journey of faith—the test to sacrifice his son Isaac. This test of faith, then, was to see whether Abraham truly trusted God that their miracle baby, Isaac, would grow up to father a great nation. Why does this matter? Because it brings out a crucial point skeptics often fail to recognize: *Abraham believed that somehow, someway, his act of obedience—even though it might mean killing Isaac—would not end with the death of his son.* As he climbed the mountain with the boy, surely his emotions would be raging as his mind wrestled with this agonizing paradox. Yet he knew Isaac was going to come back down with him. He had to. God's promise was not yet fulfilled, and Abraham believed God's promise. This isn't a tormented father preparing to say goodbye to his son forever. This is a resolved man walking in tremendous obedience because he is convinced of the promises of God.

Abraham's faith is apparent in the story itself. In Genesis 22:4-5, Abraham sees the mountain of sacrifice in the distance. So he says to his servants, "Stay here with the donkey...The boy and I will travel a little farther. *We* will worship there, and then *we* will come right back" (emphasis ours). He believed the two of them would worship God and come back down the mountain together.

As they walked on, Isaac asked Abraham about the offering. "We have the fire and the wood...but where is the sheep for the burnt offering?" (Genesis verse 7). "God will provide a sheep for the burnt offering, my son." Again, Abraham truly believed God would provide.

We pointed out in the previous chapter that the Bible does not skirt around the flaws of our faithful heroes. Abraham's life included several times of failure. We read that on two occasions before Isaac's birth, Abraham, not trusting in God, deceived a king to protect himself and his wife (Genesis 12:20). Then after years went by without the promised son being born, he and Sarah took matters into their own hands. He fathered a son by Sarah's servant, Hagar (Genesis 16:1-4).

Yet Abraham never doubted that God is good. Earlier in Genesis 18, God revealed to Abraham his plans to destroy Sodom and Gomorrah. Abraham boldly appealed to God's goodness for the innocent lives in those two cities. Doesn't it seem odd that he never appealed to God when asked to sacrifice his son? In the face of that outrageous request, Abraham was remarkably silent. Why? We suggest Abraham was silent because he saw no reason to doubt God. The Lord had proven himself faithful to Abraham time and time again.

To drive this point home, look at what Hebrews 11:17-19 says concerning Abraham's test:

> It was by faith that Abraham offered Isaac as a sacrifice when God was testing him. Abraham, who had received God's promises, was ready to sacrifice his only son, Isaac, even though God had told him, "Isaac is the son through whom your descendants will be counted." Abraham reasoned that if Isaac died, God was able to bring him back to life again. And in a sense, Abraham did receive his son back from the dead.

Once again, we have an explicit statement that Abraham had faith in the preservation of his son. Even if Isaac had died, Abraham knew he couldn't stay dead.

Understanding Abraham's faith puts his test in a new and better light. It's a lot easier to get on a plane when you know and believe the pilot can land it safely. But to be clear, Abraham's journey would still have been difficult. He knew God was going to come through, but he didn't know how. That is enough to shake a man, especially when his son's life is at stake. But God was gentle to Abraham, and Abraham was strong for God. His faith carried him through—faith that was ultimately provided by God himself.[6]

Why would God put his dearly beloved Abraham through this trying ordeal? He already knew the state of his faith prior to the test. We suggest that the experience was orchestrated primarily for Abraham's growth. First, God's test graciously provided a way for Abraham to vindicate the shame he likely felt from his previous faith blunders. Second, Abraham's stretching experience would have made him a stronger man. This would enable him to stand with confidence in the trials ahead, knowing that God will always come through for him even when nothing seems to make sense.

What About Isaac?

One other troubling detail about this story is often missed: What kind of trauma did poor Isaac endure while his father bound him and raised a knife over his throat? Wouldn't such a terrifying ordeal leave someone scarred for life? Did Isaac not struggle? Did he not scream? How could he ever again experience peace with his father after such an experience?

The Bible does not provide direct insight into this question. We know nothing of Isaac's inner turmoil or if he fought furiously against his dad until reaching a heart-wrenching moment of defeat. Our natural inclination is to assume that he would have struggled, screamed, and cried like any little boy would. That seems to be a safe assumption, right? There's only one problem with it: Isaac was not a little boy. As we will soon see, this fact makes all the difference.

The Hebrew word translated "boy" (*na'ar*) is used for a broad range of ages, from children to young adults ready for marriage. We don't know Isaac's exact age in this story, but he was at least old enough to journey for several days and climb the mountain carrying firewood.[7] We also know that Abraham was very old at the time, well over 100 years.[8] These facts give us reason to think that Isaac was not in emotional turmoil during the incident. Otherwise, he would have resisted. If he had done that, he likely would have overpowered his father and escaped. In fact, there is a strong Jewish tradition that says Isaac's faith was just as commendable as Abraham's, even postulating that Isaac requested to be bound lest he change his mind in the final moment of testing.[9] Isaac's role in this story was also noticed by the reformer Martin Luther: "There was a great light of faith in that young man…For he who believes that God is the Creator, who makes all things out of nothing, must of necessity conclude that therefore God can raise the dead."[10]

Another reason we can believe Isaac was resolute about submitting to death is because his story so closely parallels that of Christ, who resolved to die on the cross (see Galatians 3:16). Consider this: Abraham told Isaac that God would provide a *lamb*. But the story ends with Abraham sacrificing a *ram*. Our first thought is to assume that Abraham was mistaken. The truth, however, was that God had not yet finished the story. Centuries later, God would offer up his own Son—Jesus Christ—the "Lamb of God"[11] who would carry the wood of his own sacrifice[12] up a different mountain,[13] and willingly give his own life as an atonement for our sins. With this parallel in place, we have more reason to believe that Isaac's posture was similar to the posture of Jesus—submitted and willing, not tormented and resistant.

Did Isaac live the rest of his days scarred and traumatized in the presence of a father who put him through a near-death experience? Not likely. We suggest his experience would have been like that of any believer who trusts his life to God's hands when he passes away from this earth and wakes up on the other side of eternity. What a marvelous experience that will be—when faith becomes sight, when God fulfills his promise to resurrect us from the dead and welcome us home!

The Suffering of Job

Scholars classify the book of Job with the wisdom literature of Scripture, a specific genre intended to lead its readers into wisdom and to wrestle with the deep things of God. Job is a discourse about the justice of God in light of great evil and suffering in our world. The book asks tough questions about how to understand God's goodness in times of great trial. Such questions hit close to home for many of us.

The book begins by telling the story of a man named Job, who was both wealthy and blameless before God. But like any good story, happy beginnings don't last long.

> One day the members of the heavenly court came to present themselves before the LORD, and the Accuser, Satan, came with them. "Where have you come from?" the LORD asked Satan. Satan answered the LORD, "I have been patrolling the earth, watching everything that's going on."
>
> Then the LORD asked Satan, "Have you noticed my servant Job? He is the finest man in all the earth. He is blameless—a man of complete integrity. He fears God and stays away from evil."
>
> Satan replied to the LORD, "Yes, but Job has good reason to fear God. You have always put a wall of protection around him and his home and his property. You have made him prosper in everything he does. Look

how rich he is! But reach out and take away everything he has, and he will surely curse you to your face!"

"All right, you may test him," the LORD said to Satan. "Do whatever you want with everything he possesses, but don't harm him physically." So Satan left the LORD's presence (Job 1:6-12).

The story continues, and it does not go well for poor Job. As in a bad nightmare, the accuser has his way, and Job's life falls apart in rapidly descending disasters. Raiders come and take all his livestock. Fire from above destroys his flock of sheep. Even worse, a fierce wind destroys the house where Job's children are gathered, killing them all.

Remarkably, Job continues to honor God. But his trials are not over. The accuser, having lost his challenge to God, returns to the heavenly court for a second round. He chalks up Job's unshaken integrity to the fact that he still has his health. So God lets the accuser cover Job's body with a foul, unsightly, open-sored, and perpetually pain-wracking disease.

Three of Job's friends visit him during his time of loss and distress. In a remarkable display of compassion, they sit with Job in silence for seven days straight, "for they saw that his suffering was too great for words" (Job 2:13). When they finally speak, however, we do not hear the sound of wisdom. They insist that God must be punishing Job for wrongdoing, and the solution to his problems is for him to repent. But Job is certain he has not acted unjustly. This turns into a painfully long argument between Job and his friends. Over time, Job's complaints shift away from his friends and are directed toward God. Finally, God speaks:

Who is this that questions my wisdom
   with such ignorant words?

Brace yourself like a man,
    because I have some questions for you,
    and you must answer them.
Where were you when I laid the foundations of the earth?
    Tell me, if you know so much.
Who determined its dimensions
    and stretched out the surveying line?
What supports its foundations,
    and who laid its cornerstone
as the morning stars sang together
    and all the angels shouted for joy? (Job 38:2-7).

This was only the beginning. When Job asks God to answer his pain, God responds with some questions of his own—eighty-six, to be exact![14]

Here we find ourselves faced with another very troubling view of God. According to theologian Ellen Davis,

> The standoff between God and his professional Adversary looks just like a pagan folktale, where the gods vie for power and prestige, and humanity is inevitably the pawn in the game. By contrast, biblical religion is generally insistent that God does not play dice with the universe. It is shocking, therefore, to see Israel's God accept the dare…If we take that admission at face value, then God looks considerably worse than the Adversary. Maybe the [Adversary] is upholding some notion of cosmic order and fairness. But God appears to be the most vicious kind of stooge, for his cruelty is incidental and therefore utterly indefensible.[15]

From this perspective, Job's unfortunate circumstances succumb to the collateral damage of a cosmic fistfight between God and Satan. Worse yet, God's response to Job's agony sounds petty and cruel, as if to say, "Shut up. I know what I'm doing. I'm God and I'm awesome. I have infinite wisdom and you're just a lowly human. You would never understand." But from our perspective as readers, the reason for Job's suffering does not seem difficult to understand at all; it's the result of God's wager with Satan. It's no wonder God doesn't want to discuss it with Job…right?

A Theology like Job's

I (Josh) can relate somewhat to Job's suffering. Although I never had a foray of unfortunate events destroy everything I loved and worked for, I may as well have. When I set off for Kellogg College in Battle Creek, Michigan, I was angry, mad, hurt, wounded, and just plain ticked off at my parents and especially at God. Growing up, I experienced the shame and hurt of having a drunken father in a small town. I was often humiliated by the jokes about my dad making a fool of himself in front of others. Often when my father was beating on my mother, I was beating on him. On top of it all, from six to thirteen years of age, every week I was homosexually raped in my own home. My predator was a hired cook and housekeeper. Those seven years under his grip just about destroyed everything in my life. So when I went off to college, it was more to get away from home than to get an education.

In some ways, I shared a theology similar to Job's. Like him, I wanted God to give an account for why my life became riddled with so much pain. But unlike Job, I didn't merely question God; I hated him! There was no question in my mind about who was responsible for my pain.

What's Going On with This Book?

Sadly, the suffering I experienced growing up is not unusual. We live in a shattered world. Many of us have experienced horrendous pain, making it difficult to make sense of God. This is why the book of Job is so relevant for our world today. It was written to guide us through the shared experience of human suffering. But if we are stuck thinking it paints an ugly picture of God, we will miss its valuable wisdom. So who is this God we encounter in the story of Job? Is he really a petty cosmic gambler who pawns us off to win a bet with Satan?

To understand what God wants us to learn about himself in the book of Job, we first need to identify the question it encourages us to ask. Most readers turn to Job to answer the question, How could a good God allow a righteous person to suffer? This is the question we find Job's friends exploring when they begin to speak. But the conversation quickly turns into a long-winded argument, and we are left doubting whether Job and his friends are making any progress. Let's be honest: It's not an easy read! As my (Matthew's) Old Testament professor once said, "By the time you're halfway through the book of Job, you're about ready to throw your Bible against the wall!"[16] But when we pick up our Bible from the floor, smooth out its rumpled pages, and read on, we soon learn the reason for our frustration. We've been asking the wrong question. The book is priming us for a different, deeper question than the problem of pain and suffering. This question is, Where is wisdom found? It is asked in Job 28:12, the literary center of the book's structure.[17] It is here that the Bible invites us to consider a different way, the way of wisdom.

With this in mind, we are ready to understand what God is doing when he speaks to Job in chapters 38–41. God challenges Job with a long list of questions that lead Job to realize that true wisdom is found only in him. God's majesty is vividly displayed as he offers Job a God's-eye view of the order of the universe. Suddenly we see a God far more grand, far more complex, and far less predictable than the god Job and his friends have tried to stuff into their little boxes. We are introduced to a universe with trillions upon trillions of moving parts upheld by God, who is infinite wisdom.

How does Job respond to all this?

> I had only heard about you before,
>   but now I have seen you with my own eyes.
> I take back everything I said,
>   and I sit in dust and ashes to show my repentance[18] (Job 42:5-6).

Initially, Job was a long-winded man, but now he has little to say. With his eyes gazing upon the incomprehensible wisdom of God, Job admits defeat. But more than that, he finds what he truly needed all along. Job never got an answer from God; he got God himself. Suddenly his perspective is expanded even beyond the pain of his own suffering. This new perspective does not make all his problems go away, but it does make all the difference in terms of his internal peace, for now he has found resolution to his understanding of God.

Back to my (Josh's) story. Angry and hurt at God, I set out to show that Christianity was a complete fraud. But the more I examined the Bible, the more I realized I had a twisted view of God, Jesus, and what the Christian life is really like. I struggled for several months. Finally, on December 19 at 8:30 p.m., I gave in and trusted Jesus as my personal Savior and Lord. My life was forever changed. This doesn't mean all my problems went away; many of the hurts were still there. But I now had within me the Holy Spirit, who enabled me to live above them.

In addition, I have since seen how God has used some of my hurts to show how I will always need him. It was exhilarating when, months later, I actually thanked God for the way he formed me through all the suffering I endured growing up. Its impact on me was profound. It hit me hard that my loving heavenly Father permitted many of these challenges to mold me into who I am today. I would not want to change any of it. (Yet I wouldn't ever want my children to experience any of it.)

"Have you noticed my servant Job?"

God's discourse is at the heart of the book's theology. Simply put, he tells Job and his friends that his knowledge and understanding are unreachable. This is not to suggest we have nothing to say about why God allows pain and suffering. In hindsight, I (Josh) found that my own suffering played a huge role in my eventual discovery of Christ. We could also speak of how pain is not God's doing but is the result of man's free will, or of how God uses suffering to develop in us good qualities like courage and compassion. A good God has good reasons for allowing suffering to exist in this world. But at the end of the day, we will never find satisfaction in any answer. We will only find satisfaction in God. Whereas other worldviews say suffering is due to bad karma (Hinduism), or it's an illusion (Buddhism), or it's the result of natural selection playing its course in a purposeless universe (atheism), Jesus says, "Come to me, all of you who are weary and carry heavy burdens, and I will give you rest" (Matthew 11:28).

Where is wisdom to be found? It is found in God. How, then, do we find peace in our pain? By turning to him in relationship. Why can we do this? Because God is good.

In light of everything we have learned from Job's encounter with God, we are forced to reconsider our understanding of this "challenge" between God and the adversary at the beginning of this story. As readers, we initially thought we understood the cause of Job's suffering because we had the privilege of peering into the heavenly council. But now it becomes apparent that we are not much more advantaged than Job or his friends. Yes, the story shows the adversary "egging on" God to give him access to Job's life, but who was "egging on" the adversary to present his challenge? Read the introduction again and look at how it all begins. "Then the LORD asked Satan, 'Have you noticed my servant Job? He is the finest man in all the earth. He is blameless—a man of complete integrity. He fears God and stays away from evil'" (Job 1:8). God is the one playing the cards, not Satan. He knew all along how Satan would respond. This is no divine dare. God had already determined for Job to experience a season of extreme anguish before the adversary ever spoke up, and his rationale for this is beyond our ability to know fully.

And yet, the book of Job ends with some very peculiar details that give us the tiniest glimpse into the purpose of Job's suffering.

First, after God finishes correcting Job (near the end of the book), he rebukes Job's three friends for speaking poorly of him. He then instructs these friends to repent with burnt offerings and has Job pray for them. This creates an opportunity for Job and his friends to rebuild their relationships into something stronger. We also see God positioning Job as a kind of priest, a man who now has the right to minister to others because he himself was ministered to by God.

Second, the text says that all Job's brothers and sisters surrounded him with love. This would undoubtedly be a cherished memory of Job's, which he never would have experienced if not for the trouble that came his way.

Third, God restored Job's fortunes to double what he originally had. This is not to say that God will always replace stuff with stuff, but it does show the heart of our Father to give even greater blessings when we honor him through our pain. Yet something in this third point may still be troublesome. In the words of Davis,

> The note at the end of the book that Job had seven sons and three daughters is often considered to be a cheap parting shot—as though God could make it all up by giving Job another set of children to replace the ones who were lost. But that is to judge the last scene of the book from the wrong side. This book is not about justifying God's actions; it is about Job's transformation. It is useless to ask how much (or how little) it costs God to give more children. The real question is how much it costs Job to become a father again. How can he open himself again to the terrible vulnerability of loving those whom he cannot protect against suffering and untimely death?[19]

As it turns out, Job's suffering caused an expansion of his heart. Not only did he find the courage to be with his wife and have children again, but now we are introduced to the names of his daughters and his willingness to give them a portion of his inheritance among their brothers—something altogether unheard of in the culture of the time.[20] Job is a new man, forged in the fires that only suffering can produce. Even in the midst of extraordinary suffering, God can and will show himself as good.

"Have you noticed my servant Job?" This is not just a question from God to the adversary. This is a question from God to us.

6

Wise Legislator or Oppressive Dictator?

A literal reading of the Old Testament not only permits but *requires* heretics to be put to death.[1]

—SAM HARRIS

[We] need to remember that God's goodness is behind all his commands. His commands are meant to bless humans...While we have all experienced bad laws or unnecessary laws, if the lawgiver is generous and gracious, his laws will be good.[2]

—DAVID LAMB

We humans seem to have an inbred resistance to law and authority, especially in our Western individualistic culture. We don't want restrictions. We want freedom to do as we please, and we shun anyone who tells us otherwise. Slowly, over the past half-century or so, we have seen lawmakers and courts chip away at many of the restrictions US law has imposed on its citizens. One by one, laws against censorship, abortion, sexual freedom, and many others restricting controversial activities have fallen. Even now we see a demand for more laws to be abolished, as was vividly witnessed in the turmoil of 2020 and 2021. Protests turned violent and rampant lawlessness prevailed. Burning. Looting. Antagonism toward police. Anarchy. Defiance of authority.

This perpetual quest for greater freedoms and latitude for personal behavior naturally ignites outrage when people read the restrictive laws God imposed on the Israelites in the Old Testament. The first five books of the Bible, known as the Torah, Pentateuch, or Law of Moses ("law" for short), serve as the foundation of God's law to his people in Old Testament times. One Jewish rabbi counted 613 laws in the Torah.[3] To modern sensibilities, this piling up of rules seems tyrannical and intolerable. We may feel as if God is controlling, micromanaging, oppressing, forcing his people to obey all kinds of regulations, and punishing them severely if they fail to comply.

God established his law for the Israelites after he freed them from slavery in Egypt. But reading these laws can make us wonder: Were they really freed from slavery, or were they merely put in bondage to another master?

It's not just the sheer volume of these God-imposed laws that raises the question; it's also the offensive nature of so many of them. There are laws regulating the ownership of slaves. There are laws demanding exclusive worship of God alone. There are laws demanding the killing of animals for sacrifices. Many of these laws, if broken, demand the penalty of death. In this chapter, we will explore some of the most challenging aspects of God's law that we face in the Old Testament.

Why Would God Tolerate Owning Slaves?

Given how pervasive slavery was in ancient times, many of us would expect God's law for his own people would explicitly abolish slavery. It doesn't. There is no law anywhere in the Bible that says you cannot own slaves. Quite the contrary, various policies exist in the law explicitly allowing the ownership of slaves (e.g., Exodus 21:20-21; Leviticus 25:44-46). Many skeptics have used these passages to indict God for condoning slavery. Is it possible that they have a point?

Curiously, 31 percent of teens and young adults ages 13–21 strongly agree that morality changes over time with the current norms of society.[4] If this is true, then slavery in the Bible shouldn't concern us. Virtually everyone in biblical times believed slavery was morally acceptable. But if you believe, as we do, that true moral standards exist independent of time and culture, then we have reason to show concern about slavery in the Bible. We will begin by discussing slavery in the Old Testament law and conclude with a few comments about slavery in the New Testament.

When you think of slavery today, you are probably drawn back to the horrible slave trade systems of the sixteenth through nineteenth centuries. Innocent people—especially Africans— were captured and shipped like cattle to be sold as commodities primarily to markets in Europe, the Americas, and the Caribbean. This slavery was fueled by the evils of racism and power. Slavery in the Bible, however, was different. For starters, consider this passage from Deuteronomy 15:12-15 (NIV):

> If any of your people—Hebrew men or women—sell themselves to you and serve you six years, in the seventh year you must let them go free. And when you release them, do not send them away empty-handed. Supply them liberally from your flock, your threshing floor and your winepress. Give to them as the LORD your God has blessed you. Remember that you were slaves in Egypt and the LORD your God redeemed you. That is why I give you this command today.

Our first observation is that Hebrews would voluntarily sell themselves to other Hebrews. This was common practice as a way to pay off debt or a means for the poor to make a living.[5] This voluntary servitude relieved poverty and countered the threat of starvation. What else would they do? Back then, an indebted Hebrew could not pick up food stamps or draw a loan from their local bank. Rather, they volunteered for slavery on the principle that if they couldn't pay for a meal, they would go to the kitchen and clean some dishes.

This and other Old Testament laws make it clear that Hebrew slavery was not an issue of racism. In fact, the act of kidnapping a person for slavery was strictly prohibited and punishable by death (Exodus 21:16). Further, the passage above required slaves to be set free every seventh year, and the owner was to furnish the person generously from his own possessions to send him off well-provisioned.

You may be thinking that slavery in Old Testament times often seems more like servanthood. Indeed, sometimes the distinction between "slave" and "servant"[6] in the Bible is not clear. The original Hebrew word translated "slave"— 'ebed—is also the word used for "servant." Context is our guide for distinguishing between the two concepts (though sometimes the distinction is unclear). 'Ebed does not necessarily indicate a lowly or undignified position, but instead, signals a subordinate relationship. As the *Theological Dictionary of the Old Testament* states, "The [substantive] 'ebed refers to a person who is subordinated to someone else. This subordination can manifest itself in various ways, however, and 'ebed accordingly can have different meanings: slave, servant, subject, official, vassal, or "servant" or follower of a particular god."[7] Case in point: The NIV and ESV translate the plural form of 'ebed as "royal officials" in 1 Kings 1:9.

To be clear, the problem of slavery in the Bible is not yet resolved. Although some Old Testament slave laws might be better understood as indentured servant laws, Israelites could still acquire foreigners as slaves, and these people were treated as property. Consider Leviticus 25:44-46:

> You may purchase male and female slaves from among the nations around you. You may also purchase the children of temporary residents who live among you, including those who have been born in your land. You may treat them as your property, passing them on to your children as a permanent inheritance. You may treat them as slaves, but you must never treat your fellow Israelites this way.

Are we back to square one?

In antebellum America, some preachers justified slavery by claiming the Old Testament laws regulating slavery indicated God's endorsement of the practice. In first-century Judea, Pharisees who justified divorce confronted Jesus on the same basis: God must have endorsed the practice because it was regulated in the Torah. How did Jesus respond? According to Matthew 19:8, he replied, "Moses permitted divorce only as a concession to your hard hearts, but it was not what God had originally intended."

Herein lies an important principle of interpretation for understanding the law in the Old Testament. By looking at Jesus's response on divorce, we discover that in some cases, the law regulated certain activities that God did not endorse. This does not mean he got it wrong in the Old Testament, or that his moral standard changed over time. Rather, it means God's law in the Old Testament was designed to accommodate a morally corrupt people (cf. Deuteronomy 30:11). We suggest the same principle applies where the law strictly regulated the unjust practice of slavery.

We are inclined to draw this conclusion for two reasons. First, because humans were made in God's image (Genesis 1:27), they are endowed with infinite value, dignity, and worth. Second, when God chose Abraham to become the forefather of his people, his intention was for Abraham's descendants to be a blessing to the rest of the world (Genesis 12:1-3; 22:17-18). Both of these points make it unlikely God would have wanted his own people to hold others in demeaning captivity. Given the greater context of human value and God's mission for Israel, the slave regulations were far more likely to be accommodative, not inherently desirable.

Had God's law explicitly outlawed chattel slavery in a society structured around it, what do you suppose would have happened? Think back to when Abraham Lincoln issued the Emancipation Proclamation to free slaves in the Southern states of America. Not surprisingly, the South did not comply. Their economics and livelihood were structured around slave labor. Likewise, you cannot simply decree that a communist nation should become capitalist overnight. It takes a long, painful process to reorder society so profoundly. Had God outlawed slavery outright, the Israelites probably would have found the commandment too difficult and rejected it altogether. If that had happened, slavery would probably have been left completely unchecked. So what did God do? Rather than jeopardizing the Middle Eastern economy with an absolute prohibition, God created laws to help slaves trapped in their awful predicament. Slaves were required to rest on the Sabbath like everyone else (Exodus 20:10). The Hebrew slaves joined in celebrating the Passover meal (Exodus

12:44). There was protection for runaway slaves seeking asylum (Deuteronomy 23:15). There were safeguards preventing slave brutality (Exodus 21:26-27). God was quick to remind his people that they were once slaves in Egypt, but he showed kindness and set them free (Leviticus 25:38, 42; Deuteronomy 15:15). It is clear that the Old Testament law recognized slaves as human beings with fundamental human rights. This was unheard of in its time. In fact, the historian Muhammad Dandamayev says, "We have in the Bible *the first appeals in world literature* to treat slaves as human beings for their own sake and not just in the interests of their masters"[8] (emphasis ours).

The Old Testament law did not eradicate slavery, but it met the people where they were. It focused on the dignity of all human life, and it helped to create a culture in which the end of slavery might someday be obtained. For this reason, we can look straight into the slavery laws of the Old Testament and discover right in the midst of those laws that God is good.

Fast-forward to New Testament times when slavery remained rampant in Roman culture. Unlike Jews with their Old Testament law, Christians were in no position to change the government, and any commandment for slaves to run away from their masters would likely have made their lives even more difficult.[9] So, Paul wrote similar regulations to safeguard slaves and make master-slave relationships as healthy as possible (Ephesians 6:5-9).

If you want a clear insight into Paul's view on slavery, turn to the book of Philemon. In this heartfelt letter, Paul urged Philemon to welcome back a runaway slave and to treat him no longer as a slave, but as a fellow brother in Christ (Philemon 8-17).[10] What Paul said to Philemon is revealing: "You know, I *could* just lay a hard command on you to do what's right here" (verse 8, paraphrased). Instead, he chose to operate under a different system governed by love. He appealed to Philemon's conscience, trusting that God had produced in him a heart for the freedom of human life.

Is God an Egotistical Narcissist?

Deuteronomy 6:4-5 is considered to be one of the most important passages for the life of God's people. It says, "Listen, O Israel! The LORD is our God, the LORD alone. And you must love the LORD your God with all your heart, all your soul, and all your strength." Imagine your boss at work commanding you to love him or her that way. Such a person would be extremely egotistical, if not just plain sick in the head. Because God frequently commands his people to worship him through many different means, such as music, sacrificial offerings, or in this case, love, doesn't that make him seem to be a grotesquely self-absorbed egotist?

It's important to understand that human beings have a natural tendency to place their affection, attention, and admiration on exceptional people or desirable objects. Just look at how people flock to concerts, major sports events, and red-carpet galas with hands raised high or aching from applause. Even our bank account, reputation, or level of prestige can easily become an object of obsession. We may not recognize our preoccupation with performers or things as worship, but that is essentially what's happening. So when God calls for our worship, he isn't asking that we do something unnatural for us. He is asking us to redirect our focus to him.

With this perspective in place, can we say God has good reasons for directing our worship to him? Absolutely. Let's explore four of them.

First, the English word *worship* is derived from an older term, *worth-ship*.[11] The idea is that any object of worship must have the condition or quality of being worthy. The worthiness of God is the resounding message of the Bible from cover to cover. The absolute goodness of God is our underlying message in this book as well. In the words of Christian worship leader Micah Lang, "When we understand the greatness of God, the stability of His character, the perfection of His justice, the depth of His grace, the limitless nature of His love, the wonder of His holiness, and the sacrifice of His Son, it should not be difficult for us to be moved greatly in our desire to worship God, and worship Him passionately."[12]

Second, the call to worship God is to be understood like any other command in the Bible: It is for our good. We might say that throughout the Bible, human flourishing is presented as a worshipful life in the presence of God.[13] This explains why worship is connected with blessing (Exodus 23:25-26; Deuteronomy 11:13-15), guidance (Acts 13:2-3), deliverance (Acts 16:25-26), and especially joy (Psalms 43:4; 47:1; 95:1; Colossians 3:16). Given these benefits of worship, why wouldn't a good God repeatedly urge us to direct our adoration toward him?

Third, God is not arrogant for commanding us to worship him any more than a drill sergeant is arrogant for instructing his cadets to obey his orders. In both cases, the justification for the command comes from the relative position of both parties. As the creator of the universe, whom Scripture defines as infinitely powerful, majestic, and glorious, God has perfect rationale for summoning our worship. His unique status in relationship with us places him in a rightful and deserved position to be worshipped—a position no fellow human can occupy.

Fourth, God does not merely ask his people to worship him, but he opens our hearts that we might receive this instruction gladly. In Jeremiah 32:39-40, God said,

> I will give them one heart and one purpose: to worship me forever, for their own good and for the good of all their descendants. And I will make an everlasting covenant with them: I will never stop doing good for them. I will put a desire in their hearts to worship me, and they will never leave me.

This statement, originally spoken for the benefit of the Israelites, extends forward to God's church, whose members have become a part of his global family. We find this desire to worship God to be present in our own lives and in the lives of other committed Christians. We worship God because he deposited that desire within us when we first placed our trust in him.

Are We Really Supposed to Fear God?

Ben Bennett and I (Josh) recently published a book titled *Free to Thrive: How Your Hurt, Struggles, and Deepest Longings Can Lead to a Fulfilling Life.* Both of us came to the topic as people who have experienced significant emotional wounds, not the least of which were father issues. As I shared in the previous chapter, my father was a town drunk who would frequently beat my mom to a bloody mess. Ben shared that his father's frequent bursts of anger led to feelings of inadequacy and even concern for his safety. In both cases, our fathers were *frightening* people. With stories like ours, it was difficult to peel away our negative experiences with earthly fathers in order to understand God as a loving father. But when the Bible encourages God's people to fear him, as it does in at least 274 verses,[14] we might begin to wonder why. Is it possible he's no better than the abusive fathers we grew up with?

Here are just a few examples of the command to fear God (taken from various translations):

- Deuteronomy 6:13 (NIV)—"Fear the LORD your God, serve him only and take your oaths in his name."
- Psalm 2:11 (ESV)—"Serve the LORD with fear, and rejoice with trembling."
- Isaiah 8:13 (NLT)—"Make the LORD of Heaven's Armies holy in your life. He is the one you should fear. He is the one who should make you tremble."
- 2 Corinthians 5:11 (NASB)—"Therefore, knowing the fear of the Lord, we persuade people."
- 1 Peter 2:17 (KJV)—"Honour all men. Love the brotherhood. Fear God. Honour the king."
- Acts 9:31 (CSB)—"So the church throughout all Judea, Galilee, and Samaria had peace and was strengthened. Living in the fear of the Lord and encouraged by the Holy Spirit, it increased in numbers."

Some say that to fear God is simply to have a sense of awe, wonder, reverence, and respect toward him. But if that's all it really is, why does almost every English translation of the Bible still render the term as "fear" and not "revere" or "respect"?[15] The reason is that of all the English words to choose from, "fear" is still most fitting to describe this curious biblical concept in most contexts. It's not a perfect translation, but it's close.

In Exodus 19, we read of God descending on a mountain in the form of fire accompanied by thunder and lightning. The

Israelites who witnessed this display did not gather at the mountain as if around a nice campfire and sing "Kumbaya." No, they trembled in fear (Exodus 20:18). So Moses, their leader, said to them, "Do not be afraid. God has come to test you, so that the fear of God will be with you to keep you from sinning" (Exodus 20:20 NIV).

What? Did you read that correctly? Did Moses tell the people *not to fear so that they might fear?* Yes. Evidently, the Bible presents a wrong way to fear God and a right way to fear him. In our Western culture, we tend to view fear in only one way—as a negative thing. But the ancients viewed fear more broadly.[16] The author of Ecclesiastes considered fearing God to be the most meaningful thing we could do with our lives (Ecclesiastes 5:7; 12:13).

We are so far removed from this mode of thinking that the fear of God is a difficult concept to fully appreciate. But to imagine that biblical authors would actually want us to see God as a tyrannical bully who manipulates people with fear tactics is even more difficult. No devout author of Scripture would ever mean to communicate this, and no devout Jewish community would ever receive such a crazy notion in their collection of Scripture. These injunctions to fear God must have been written to communicate something different than our natural understanding of fear in the modern world. We are therefore compelled by reason to reconsider whether fearing God casts a negative shadow on his character.

When we think this through, we realize that not all fear is negative. We even speak of "healthy fear" because we understand that fear can be useful in leading us to make wise choices. Consider a loving father who orders his child not to play in the street. With a stern face, he strictly warns, "If you play in the street, I'll have to punish you." The child stays out of the street for fear of the father's punishment. But in time and through experience, the child comes to learn that the father's inducement to fear was motivated by his love. Similarly, God hopes to instill a sense of healthy fear in our hearts to keep us from making poor decisions contrary to his commandments—all of which are given for our good.

We hope you can see that to fear God does not mean our relationship with him is unhealthy, abusive, strained, or damaged. Several passages of Scripture clearly imply otherwise. Psalm 25:14 says, "The LORD is a friend to those who fear him." Psalm 103:17 says, "The love of the LORD remains forever with those who fear him." Even some of the verses we listed earlier imply a connection between fear and joy or encouragement. Although fear kept the Israelites trembling at a distance from Mount Sinai, the author of Hebrews taught that because of Jesus, we can boldly approach God. This contrasts the Israelites' terrifying experience at the fiery, thundering Sinai with an intensely close and personal relationship with him at the new and glorious Mount Zion (Hebrews 10:19-22; 12:18-29).

That's a Lot of Death!

Another challenging aspect of God's law is its liberal imposition of the death penalty. The crimes that demand execution are many. To name a few:

- Being a sorceress (Exodus 22:18)
- Having sexual intercourse with an animal (Exodus 22:19)
- Profaning/working on the Sabbath (Exodus 31:14-15; 35:2)

- Involvement with adultery (Leviticus 20:10)
- Sexual intercourse with one's parents or one's children (Leviticus 20:11-12)
- Blasphemy/speaking irreverently about God (Leviticus 24:15-16)
- Taking another human life (Leviticus 24:17)
- Unauthorized touching of holy things (Numbers 4:15)

To be frank, God's broad application of the death penalty is a hard pill to swallow, especially in cases where the offense seems trivial. You will be relieved, however, to learn that some aspects of Old Testament law may not be quite as rigid as they first seem.

There are about fifteen offenses in the law that require the death penalty. One instance, however, adds an additional detail that may shed new light on all the others. In the case of premeditated murder, the law stipulates that no ransom or substitute penalty will be allowed (Numbers 35:31). Evidently, such a substitutionary penalty was available for other infractions requiring the death penalty.[17] Instead of suffering death, the offender could pay a fine. If this were indeed a possibility, it certainly would have been the norm!

John Goldingay has argued that the law's imposition of such strict punishment was a way the ancient writers highlighted the seriousness of an offense. In his words:

The title "the Law" for these five books is a misleading translation of the word Torah, which means "instruction" or "teaching." And it's generally misleading to think of its individual sections of teaching as "laws," as if they were like Western state law or canon Law. A concrete indication of that fact within the Old

Testament itself is that one can find little match between the prescriptions the Torah lays down and the way Israel actually handles offenses such as murder, idolatry, and adultery…Even faithful, Torah-keeping leaders don't treat the Torah as a statute book. They know they are not supposed to be literalistic in interpreting these "laws."

Goldingay goes on to say that this phenomenon is not unique to the Bible but was normal among other Middle Eastern peoples. He says,

When a king lays down a set of statutes, it doesn't mean they become the basis of legal practice. They are rather a collection of indications of the kind of moral and social norms that the king claims to be committed to. The Old Testament operates on a parallel basis. "Laws" that prescribe execution for murder, adultery, idolatry, and a long list of other acts are markers of the kind of religious, moral, and social commitments that God expects his people to accept. They are indications of how serious these offenses are. They comprise teaching on theological ethics in the form of laws. Understood this way, the Torah becomes more obviously useful for an understanding of Old Testament ethics.[18]

Goldingay does well to emphasize that the law of God allowed some leniency, unlike the strict nature of the traditional laws in Western nations (cf. Leviticus 10:12-20). But we should be careful not to take this observation too far. Numbers 15:32-36 is one clear example that the death penalty really was imposed in Old Testament times. We also know the Jewish leaders in New

Testament times were quick to execute others for blasphemy—just ask Jesus!

At the end of the day, our most important piece of this puzzle comes from our discussion earlier in this book about the judgment of God. We learned how God shows himself as good by punishing evil, either directly or through human agency. We recognized that God's punishment often seems excessively severe, but this is largely due to the reality of his holiness. Although God's holiness is a good thing, it puts sinful humanity in a bad spot.

The Challenge of Animal Cruelty

Some people are offended by God's law because it demands the killing of innocent animals. How could a good God create a legal system that includes ritual animal sacrifice? Shouldn't this practice be denounced as animal cruelty?

It's important for us—especially our Christian readers—to recognize that all animal life has value. Although the Bible does not recognize equal status between humans and animals,[19] they are all part of God's beautiful creation. When God made fish and birds and land animals, he saw that they were "good" (Genesis 1:21, 25). This proclamation of value set the context for how humanity was to rule over the animals, as we were charged to do in verse 28. When Balaam physically abused his donkey in Numbers 22, God spoke through the donkey to rebuke Balaam. When God's people were commanded to rest on the Sabbath, their livestock were to rest with them.[20] All this goes to show that animals are to be treated with care and respect.

Most people are comfortable with eating meat, even though it involves the killing of animals. Many people go hunting. Animal skins and other animal parts are still used for beneficial purposes. The most common prerequisite for these uses is that the animal is to be killed humanely (shame on us if it isn't!), and the animal's life is not to be wasted. Both of these points were affirmed within Israel's sacrificial system.

The animals to be sacrificed were killed by cutting their throat.[21] This procedure would have caused the greatest amount of blood loss, killing the animal as quickly and humanely as possible in that time. We can be thankful that modernity has given us better options for killing animals, but if bleeding is needed, cutting the neck is still recommended as the most humane way to do it.[22]

Furthermore, almost all the sacrificial procedures prescribed in the Bible involved eating the meat of the sacrificed animal (but not its fat).[23] So we also see that the life of the animal was not wasted. When we understand the rich symbolism and deep impact of the Old Testament sacrificial rituals, we realize that even if the meat had not been eaten, the animal was not wasted. Animal sacrifice provided a way for humanity to be provisionally reconciled with God. The sacrifice of animals demonstrated that sin was such a serious offense against a holy God that it demanded death by the shedding of blood (Hebrews 9:22). So God was gracious to allow the Israelites to offer animals as a substitute instead of themselves. Eventually, he would end the necessity of animal sacrifice by offering himself instead, which is a subject we will address in a later chapter.

Don't Tell Me How to Live My Life!

Even if we have helped you to understand some of the challenging aspects of God's law, you may feel that we have not addressed the broader complaint against God raised in the opening of this chapter: that the scope and multiple prohibitions of his law show him to be a cosmic killjoy. The Ten Commandments, for example, consist mostly of rules that say, "You can't do this." Almost everyone agrees that some degree of law is necessary to maintain a stable society. But today's emphasis on personal freedom and maximum pleasure makes many feel that God's laws are needlessly strict and tyrannically oppressive.

Everyone who has been a loving parent knows that what seems oppressive can actually be loving. Parents lay out rules for their children to protect them and train them to achieve the most rewarding life possible. Think back to the father who warned his child not to play in the street. The child may have felt frustrated, calling the rule unfair. But the father's prohibition was not arbitrary or imposed simply to exercise his control over the child. It was established out of love, to protect the child.

Similarly, God's commandments to Israelite society were given for their own good, and his commandments today are given for our own good. As Moses said in Deuteronomy 10:13 (csb): "Keep the Lord's commands and statutes I am giving you today, *for your own good*" (emphasis ours). Like the child confined to the safety of his back yard, we don't always see the purpose of the restriction. But God knows us better than we know ourselves, and his laws are designed to enable us to flourish and thrive. As Cornelius Plantinga Jr. remarked, "Everything sin touches begins to die, but we do not focus on that. We see only the vitality of the parasite, glowing with stolen life."[24]

Consider the Ten Commandments in Exodus 20. These commandments mark the beginning and the foundation of the Old Testament law. In fact, many scholars understand Deuteronomy (Moses's retelling of the law to the next generation) to be structured in ten parts, each part as an expansive commentary on one of the commandments.[25] The commandments are:

- Have no other gods but the one true God.
- Do not worship idols.
- Do not misuse the name of God.
- Keep the Sabbath (i.e., take a day of rest with God once every week).
- Honor your father and mother.
- Do not murder.
- Do not commit adultery.
- Do not steal.
- Do not give false testimony against your neighbor.
- Do not desire your neighbor's possessions.[26]

What would happen if every society in the world kept these commandments? Would we be better off? This isn't a trick question.

If you haven't already, we encourage you to read through God's Old Testament laws yourself. You will quickly notice that many of them fight for the equality of all human life. Read the laws in Exodus 23 and discover God's heart for justice and for the poor. Read the laws in Deuteronomy 24 and discover God's heart to protect widows and foreigners. Read the laws in Deuteronomy 15 and discover God's heart for generosity. Read the laws in Leviticus 19 and discover God's heart for the elderly, for honest business, for fair pay, for the deaf and the blind. Jesus was absolutely right when he said the entirety of God's law could be summed up in the command to love God and love your neighbor (Matthew 22:34-40).

With just a little reflection, we can see the benefit of God's laws even in some of the most heated areas of distrust for his Word. My (Josh's) son, Sean, once made this very pointed statement when he asked his audience to imagine a world where everyone followed God's design for sex and marriage. "There would be no sexually transmitted diseases. No abortions. No brokenness from divorce. Every child would have a father and a mother and experience the love and acceptance each parent uniquely offers. There would be no rape, no sex abuse, no sex trafficking, no pornography, and no need for a 'Me too' campaign."[27]

Rather than complaining that God is an oppressive killjoy, maybe it's time we recognize these commandments reflect a grander vision for society than we could ever attain by relying on our own wisdom.

7

How Law Became Life

It would be merely boring and idiotic to wonder
how the designer of all things conceived such a versa-
tile creature [the pig] and then commanded
his higher-mammal creation to avoid it altogether
or risk his eternal displeasure.[1]

—CHRISTOPHER HITCHENS

The heart of the matter is this: Does the God who
created us also know how to speak to us? Is He able to
communicate truth to us through words in a way that is
meaningful and understandable? The answer assumed
on every page of Scripture is "yes."[2]

—KEVIN DEYOUNG AND TED KLUCK

E ven after discovering the goodness of God within the challeng
ing aspects of his law, we may still find its endless lists of dos
and don'ts obnoxious and weird. Let's face it: Most Christian readers find it laborious to read through Leviticus and Numbers with all
their instructions about tabernacle construction, animal sacrifice,
cleanliness, disease control, seasonal procedures, etc. We may look
back on those times and wonder how the Old Testament Israelites
even tolerated being under the law.

Actually, they did more than just tolerate God's law. They celebrated it. The longest chapter in the Bible (Psalm 119, which contains 176 verses) is structured as a giant praise song celebrating the value of God's law. To state the obvious: *Someone wrote this!* Apparently, those who lived under the law found it to be not only beneficial but also beautiful and praiseworthy.

How could this be? How could the Israelite community receive God's law with such gladness of heart? Is there something essential about the nature of God's law that we are missing?

For those whose appetite is whetted to know more, we have inserted this chapter as a sort of bonus. Unlike all other chapters in the book, it's not focused on addressing complaints or objections to God based on biblical incidents or commands. Our purpose is merely to inspire you to see God and his dealings with us as they truly are—sensibly designed for our good.

Making Sense of the Garden

In order to understand the law of God, we need first to understand two things: the Garden of Eden and the ancient Israelite tabernacle. Our quest starts in Genesis 1–3, where it all began. These first few chapters of the Bible tell us how God made the cosmos, the earth, and the Garden of Eden, where he placed the first two people, Adam and Eve. The creation story gives us more than just an interesting history lesson; it is rich with theology, telling us much about the nature of God and his purpose for humankind.

Two details in this story warrant our attention. First, God is remarkably present with Adam and Eve in the garden, speaking directly to them on several occasions (Genesis 1:28-30; 2:16-17). We also find, in Genesis 3, when God walked around in the garden to look for them, Adam was familiar with the sound of his coming (Genesis 3:9-11). Even from the first few pages of the Bible, it's apparent God desires a close relationship with his people.

Second, the creation story overflows with *life*. It says God created Adam and gave him the "breath of life," enabling him to become a "living creature" (Genesis 2:7). Adam named his wife Eve, a word that sounds like "to live" in Hebrew,[3] because she would become "the mother of all living" (Genesis 3:20 ESV). The story tells of God making all kinds of plants spring up from the ground, including the "tree of life" (Genesis 2:9). The abundance of life is visualized by a river flowing out of Eden to water the garden (verse 10), and the garden itself provides rich imagery of life teeming everywhere. When God made life on Earth, he didn't hold back!

These two things—the relational presence of God and the abundance of life—are inseparably connected in the Bible.[4] Psalm 16:11 (ESV) says, "You make known to me the path of life; in your presence there is fullness of joy; at your right hand are pleasures forevermore." We are even encouraged to think of the eternal paradise in this way. Revelation 21 introduces us to the heavenly city. Although the city is glorious and huge, its defining feature is the presence of God, and it's a place reserved for those whose names are written in the book of life. So the Bible begins and ends with life in the presence of God. This garden called Eden (a name that sounds remarkably close to the Hebrew word for "delight"[5]) was the original model of paradise. But then everything went wrong.

As we noted earlier in this book, Adam and Eve disobeyed God's commandment, violating his good will for their lives by eating from the forbidden tree. As a result, they experienced proper judgment from a holy God—pain during childbirth for the woman and wearisome labor for the man. But there was another judgment far more significant: Adam and Eve were expelled from the garden.[6]

It is both fascinating and heartbreaking to see how quickly sin continued to infest human life. One chapter after Adam and Eve were expelled, their son killed his own brother, "left the LORD's presence," and settled "east of Eden" (Genesis 4:16), suggesting that he went even farther from the garden than his parents.[7] Sin continued on through Noah's sons and their descendants, through Abraham, Isaac, and Jacob. Meanwhile, the voice of God became less and less frequent through each passing generation. In the words of theologian, Michael Morales, "Broadly, Genesis moves from the life-giving Presence of God in Eden (Gen. 2–3) to the death and burial of Joseph in Egypt (Gen. 50:26)—that is, from the heights of Eden upon the mountain of God down to Sheol, the grave."[8]

Making Sense of the Tabernacle

Despite humanity's continual rebellion against God, God is not giving up on humanity. Like a dedicated husband pursuing his unfaithful wife to win her back, God is committed to being in relationship with his people. Whereas most ancient religions of that time were about people competing for the attention of their gods, the God of Israel, Isaac, and Jacob said in Exodus 19:9, "I will come to you." As we will soon see, these five words define what the tabernacle is all about.[9]

True to his word, God came to his people. After freeing the Israelites from Egyptian slavery, he led them to Mount Sinai, where he descended in a thick cloud and issued instructions for building the tabernacle. This was to be a tent, a mobile temple, for God to inhabit. It was his initial step toward reversing the damage of sin and being with his people once more. Moses drained a lot of ink to describe how the tabernacle was to be built and how it would look. To the undiscerning reader, these instructions may seem to be a long and tedious list of irrelevant details to skip over. But a careful design is only fitting for a special place, and many of the tabernacle's details were devised to match heavenly realities, as we will soon see.

Never has the presence of God been so pronounced since the Garden of Eden. Both the garden and the tabernacle served as unique locales for God's presence. This is no literary accident. As many scholars point out, the tabernacle and the garden are closely connected. Consider this:

- Both the Garden of Eden and the tabernacle have an eastward orientation.[10]

- The description of God walking about in the garden (Genesis 3:8) is used again to describe how God conducts himself in his new dwelling place (Leviticus 26:12).

- The only mentions of cherubim in the Torah are in connection with the garden (Genesis 3:24) and the tabernacle (Exodus 25–26).

- The menorah in the tabernacle appears to represent the tree of life in the garden.[11]

- The pair of verbs used to describe Adam's work in the garden in Genesis 2:15 are the same verbs used to describe Levites' work in the tabernacle (Numbers 3:7-8; 18:5-7).

More comparisons could be made.[12] Our point in all of this is to show that God's gift of the tabernacle initiates a return to the garden, and hence, a return back to life and the relational presence of God. Consider Aaron's duty inside the tabernacle in Numbers 8:1-4. Aaron was to set up the seven lamps to give light in front of the lampstand. Like many passages in the law, we may wonder about the rationale for such a curious procedure. Commentator Gordon Wenham provides great insight:

> The meaning of this action becomes apparent when the design of the holy place is taken into account. If the light beamed forwards, it would have fallen on the table of shewbread, where twelve loaves of bread, symbolizing the twelve tribes of Israel, were heaped up (Lev. 24:5-9). Light and fire represent the life-giving presence and blessing of God (e.g. Exod. 13:21-22). Thus Aaron had to arrange the lamps so that their light always illuminated the shewbread. This arrangement portrayed visually God's intention that his people should live continually in his presence and enjoy the blessing mediated by his priests.[13]

In other words, "The arrangement of the holy place of the tabernacle, therefore, portrayed the ideal of Israel basking in the light of the divine Presence in the house of God, abiding in the fires of his glory."[14]

Exodus closes with the glory of God filling the tabernacle. This may seem like a fitting end to the Torah story, but the tension has not been completely resolved. For it says in Exodus 40:35, "Moses could no longer enter the Tabernacle because the cloud had settled down over it." Although Exodus ends with a step in the right direction, not even Moses is able to approach the glory of God. Something needs to happen. That *something* is the law of God.

Making Sense of the Law of God

Although some English translations omit it, the first word of Leviticus is the word "and."[15] Clearly, the second movement of the Torah (Exodus) was meant to flow directly into the third movement (Leviticus). The story is not complete. If God's plan to dwell among his people is going to work, he needs more than a house for himself. He must create a system whereby sinful people can become fit to approach him. This is what Leviticus, God's law, is all about.

It's easy to wonder why any of this would truly be necessary. Sure, God is holy, but couldn't he have come up with some solution less burdensome or complicated than the law? Think about it this way: If you were invited to dine with the Grand Duke of Luxembourg at a prestigious dinner party and the only instructions you received included the place, the time, and to "wear a nice shirt," you might wonder if the organizers of this event will be wandering about at the next local job fair. For the sake of honor, you would expect—and even desire—detailed instructions about how to introduce yourself, how early to arrive, what to wear, proper etiquette, how to address the duke, etc.

God is not just royalty. When you approach God, you approach the divine, and he has established a fixed order for how the divine realm works. When we approach God, we are called to conform to this order, addressing issues of holiness, sinfulness, cleanliness, profanity, blood, life, death, etc. As humans, we don't have access to the deep things of God, and so the rationale behind *everything* he requires cannot be fully understood. Suffice it to say that God, in his infinite knowledge, has ordered divine reality in such a way that it would bring him maximum glory and bring us maximum good. As C.S. Lewis once remarked: "Reality, in fact, is usually something you could not have guessed. That is one of the reasons I believe Christianity. It is a religion you could not have guessed. If it offered us just the kind of universe we had always expected, I should feel we were making it up."[16]

Still, there is a lot we can discover when we dig into how God made a way to dwell among his people. Let's look at how Leviticus, the heart of God's law, is organized.

1. The Offerings

Leviticus begins by discussing the various types of offerings God's people can give (1–7). The first three types are voluntary and provide ways for the people to enjoy fellowship with God through worship and prayers of request. The fact they were optional demonstrates that these offerings were not tedious rituals performed begrudgingly. Rather, they were given by God's grace to help show humanity how to relate to him. The peace offering, which involved the sacrifice of an animal, even included a nice meal afterward.

Many of these offerings were sacrificial in nature, especially if they related to cleansing people of their sins. This may sound terribly deathly to our ears, but these sacrifices were actually about preserving life. Sin brings death to humans (Romans 6:23), so blood—representing life—was required to restore humanity to life. As God said in Leviticus 17:11, "The life of the body is in its blood. I have given you the blood on the altar to purify you, making you right with the LORD. It is the blood, given in exchange for a life, that makes purification possible."

To be clear, "It is not possible for the blood of bulls and goats to take away sins" (Hebrews 10:4). Rather, the sacrificial system prescribed in the law pointed forward to the ultimate sacrifice, that of Jesus Christ on the cross. The animal sacrifices of

Leviticus "worked" only by means of representing the blood of Jesus, which would retroactively cleanse the Israelites from their sins. So, when the Israelites sacrificed their animals, purification of sins *did* take place, but it wasn't directly through the blood of the animal. It was through the blood of Christ, which is what the blood of the animal represented.

Quality commentaries on Leviticus can help provide rationales for many of the procedural requirements of the offerings.[17] For instance:

- Why did the burnt offering require a male? (Leviticus 1:3). Probably because these sacrifices were intended to benefit the people, and males were more expendable. A herd could continue to multiply with only a few males.

- Why must the internal organs and legs be washed? (Leviticus 1:9). Probably so that no dung is present as the parts are being offered to God.

- Why would the animal be killed on the north side of the altar? (Leviticus 1:11). Probably because that is where the priest would have the most room to work within the courtyard of the tabernacle.

- Why is the pigeon alternative not mentioned for peace offerings when it is mentioned for the burnt offerings and sin offerings? Probably because the peace offering ended in a meal, and a pigeon would not supply enough meat.

- Why were the Israelites not allowed to eat the fat of the sacrifice? (Leviticus 3:17). Probably because the fat was considered the finest part, and it would be most suiting to offer it to God.

- Why must a grain offering to God not contain leaven? (Leviticus 2:4). Probably because leaven was fermented dough used in ancient times to make bread rise,[18] and fermentation represented corruption.

2. The Purification Laws

After setting out the offering procedures, Leviticus describes the ordination of Aaron as the high priest and his sons as priests. Sacrifices are offered during this time to purify these men. This section ends with the glory of God appearing before all the people as they shout for joy (Leviticus 9:23-24). Eden regained! But then tragedy strikes as two of Aaron's sons approach God with improper sacrifices. The holiness of God is violated, and the offending priests are immediately killed. Hence, we discover that although God has made a way for his people to approach him, this new way entails a real danger. As Morales puts it, "The... bridge of communication between the sacred and the profane also entails the possibility of muddling the division between them."[19] But God isn't giving up. He is committed to life and fellowship with his people. So, by his grace, God delivers the purification laws.

The purification laws include an extensive list of clean and unclean things. For someone or something to be unclean is not the same as being sinful, or even necessarily bad. *Unclean* simply means *unfit* for the things dedicated to holiness or allowed in the presence of God. Although sin leads to uncleanliness,[20] not all uncleanliness is a result of sin.[21] If we fail to recognize this, we make the mistake of thinking God is somehow morally offended when a woman is unclean for having children or when a man is unclean for having a discharge from sexual intercourse. Many (though not all) of these things have nothing morally wrong with them, but they simply don't belong in the realm of God's holy presence. Because of this, God graciously identified what is unclean in his eyes and how to find remedies for them so that his people might continue to dwell in his life-giving presence.

Still, these purification laws can be frustrating to read because of the seemingly arbitrary lists of clean and unclean things. For example, Leviticus 11:3-4 says, "You may eat any animal that has completely split hooves and chews the cud. You may not, however, eat the following animals that have split hooves or that chew the cud, but not both." Leviticus 11:20-21 says, "You must not eat winged insects that walk along the ground; they are detestable to you. You may, however, eat winged insects that walk along the ground and have jointed legs so they can jump."

What on earth is going on here?

Over the years, several suggestions have been proposed as to the meaning of these laws. It is often said they served as a way for God to make Israel distinct among the other nations.[22] Sometimes the purification laws had health and/or sanitary benefits.[23] Paul Copan observed that the unclean animals tend to be either predatorial or weak, neither of which represent what God would desire of his people.[24]

Of all the different explanations that have been given for God's purification laws, perhaps the best starting point is to remember what the garden, the tabernacle, and the law are all about—life in the presence of God. As Morales observes, "Many of the unclean animals are associated with death in some fashion, whether in being carnivorous predators or scavengers, living in caves (tombs), or, like pigs, by being associated with underworld deities in pagan worship."[25] He goes on to say, "The need to separate life from death, the unclean from the holy, also helps to explain why, for example, the high priest must never have contact with death, corpses defile, and a young goat is not to be cooked in its mother's milk."[26] Earlier, we pointed out that life is in the blood, so we also have rationale for why a woman would become unclean after the blood loss of bearing children (Leviticus 12:7). Diseases naturally convey corruption and death, so there are purification laws about leprosy (Leviticus 14). God, who constitutes the ultimate place of life, will have nothing to do with death, or even the things that represent it.

3. The Day of Atonement

At the center of the Torah is Leviticus, and at the center of Leviticus is the Day of Atonement.[27] This special day is described for us in chapter 16, after the list of the purification laws. The Day of Atonement was the one day of the year when the high priest was required to enter the most sacred place of the tabernacle, the inner sanctum, the holy of holies, where God dwelt. Through this sacred ritual, the high priest would cleanse the sins of the entire nation of Israel, as well as cleansing the tabernacle from the pollution of these sins. This culminating addition to the offerings and purification laws served as one large sweep to wipe God's people clean from impurity. The Day of Atonement was more than just another measure of safety enabling Israel to approach the holiness of God; it was the ultimate demonstration to the Old Testament believers that God was among his people, blessing them with his presence. This was how the one true living God of this universe opened a way to dwell among sinful humanity.

For those of us who appreciate the work of Christ, it should not be hard to appreciate the Day of Atonement. The parallels are striking. This special day involved the sending of one animal into the wilderness and the retaining of another animal to be sacrificed. Similarly, Jesus and Barabbas were presented before the Roman governor. Barabbas was set free, and Jesus was killed (Matthew 26:16-26). Washings and sacrifices on the Day of Atonement involved blood and water, the symbols of redemption and life. Similarly, blood and water would pour from the side of Jesus after the completion of his ultimate sacrifice (John 19:34). As the high priest entered the holy of holies, he would come before God to cleanse the people of their sins. Similarly, Hebrews 8–9 says that the resurrected Jesus, our new high priest, comes into the eternal holy of holies in heaven on behalf of the world. Simply put, the Day of Atonement *bleeds* the amazing grace of Jesus, who himself bled on our behalf.

It would be wrong to say that the Day of Atonement is the ultimate end of Leviticus. Rather, it is the ultimate beginning. Everything prior concerns God's plan to allow humanity to dwell in his presence. Everything afterward concerns how to live as a people of God. This includes instructions for various festivals and holidays, rules for holy living, judicial practices, and so on. Now that God has opened the way, he maps out what this way is meant to look like. This map continues to be drawn in the book of Numbers and is displayed with fresh life for the next generation of believers in Deuteronomy.

Was God's Law a Setup for Failure?

In Romans 5:20, Paul says, "God's law was given so that all people could see how sinful they were." Likewise, in Galatians 3:19, he says the law was given "to show people their sins." How does this idea "that the purpose of the law is to reveal humanity's sin" fit into our discussion of the law?

Some have taken Paul's statements to mean that the requirements of the law were intentionally designed to be impossible to meet, thus functioning as a proof or "gotcha" for why the atoning sacrifice of Jesus would be necessary. But wouldn't it be grossly unfair of God to deliberately create an impossible law and then punish humanity for failing to keep it? After all, the Israelites were exiled in the eighth and sixth centuries BC because they failed to keep the law despite relentless pleas from God for them to repent and return. Are we really saying this was all one big charade?

It is clear from Scripture, even before the law's establishment in Exodus 20, that humanity is born into a sinful nature and desperately needs a savior. Because of this, no law of God could possibly be fully obeyed. But to say that God created an "impossible" law is misleading. It puts the problem on the law rather than humanity's predicament with sin.

Moses, after recounting the entirety of the law, said in Deuteronomy 30:11,[28] "This commandment that I command you today is not too hard for you, neither is it far off" (ESV). From accommodations for the poor who couldn't afford the required offerings (Leviticus 5:7-13), to the leniency toward divorce because of hardened hearts (Matthew 19:8), it's clear that humanity's inability to keep the law was not because the law was rigged. In fact, the central aspect of God's law was the sacrificial system and the Day of Atonement, explicitly designed to address the people's sin (Leviticus 16:30-34).

As we have iterated throughout this chapter, God gave the law as a way for his people to have access to his presence. This isn't the same kind of presence experienced by New Testament believers, but it was aimed in that direction.[29] This shows us that in its essence, the law was intended for life with God. But the law also created an opportunity for disobedience. Thus, sin deprived the law of its life-giving purpose, just as it had robbed

Adam and Eve of the life-sustaining garden. It became clear that because of sin, the people were unwilling to follow the law, even after all of the law's accommodations. Hence, sin made the law *as death to them.* This is what Paul picks up on when he says the law was given to expose our sin. He fleshes out this concept further in Romans 7, being very careful to distinguish the goodness of the law from the infection of sin. According to Pauline scholar Frank Thielman, "Paul points out carefully that nothing he has said should lead to the conclusion that the Law and sin are identical (Rom 7:7). To the contrary, the Law is holy, righteous, good and spiritual (Rom 7:12, 14; cf. 7:22); it is only so closely allied with sin because it shows sin for the evil transgression that it is and condemns the transgressor."[30] Thankfully, the law's life-giving intention was finally realized in full when Jesus fulfilled the law on our behalf (Matthew 5:17-20; Romans 8:2-4).

In summary, the law served a dual purpose. On the one hand, it created an opportunity for God to dwell among his people. This is the immediate context of the law as revealed to us in Genesis through Deuteronomy. But on the other hand, Paul sees what the law ended up becoming in hindsight—namely, a signal pointing to our need for something even better that could never be corrupted by sin.

Even still, the law holds extraordinary value for Christians today. As we have seen in these last two chapters, it reveals the holiness of God and shows how sin alienates us from his life-giving presence. It shows what God cares about in society. It shows that God is dedicated to the protection of human life. But more than anything, it shows that God is relentless in pursuit of relationship. It shows that God is good.

8

Are Women Second-Class Christians?

The Old Testament, as Christians condescendingly
call it, has woman cloned from man for his use
and comfort. The New Testament has Saint Paul
expressing both fear and contempt for the female.
Throughout all religious texts, there is a primitive
fear that half the human race is simultaneously defiled
and unclean, and yet is also a temptation to
sin that is impossible to resist.[1]

—CHRISTOPHER HITCHENS

Under the [Hebrew] system the position of woman
was in marked contrast with her status in surrounding heathen nations. Her liberties were greater, her
employments more varied and important, her social
standing more respectful and commanding.[2]

—DWIGHT M. PRATT

A story is told of a young woman named Thecla who lived in the period of the early church. It is said that while Paul was travel-ing, Thecla heard him preach, and his message of Christ shook her to the core. Forsaking her old life, she abandoned her family and her fiancé to learn more about God through Paul. Her journeys led to extreme levels of persecution. By her own mother's request, she was publicly set on fire, but her body never burned and she emerged unscathed, delivered by the power of God. A year later, she was thrown naked into an arena with wild animals, but they did not touch her. Thecla's story is one of bravery, heroism, and total abandonment to God in the midst of great loss and persecution. She is regarded as a saint who proclaimed the gospel before great leaders and was said to have healed the sick through prayer.

The adventures of Thecla are recorded in *The Acts of Paul,* a second-century narrative that purports to tell more about the missionary journeys of Paul and those who rubbed shoulders with him. Christian scholars understand that the writing contains a great deal of legend, making it hard to determine the accuracy of Thecla's history or if she even existed.[3] Nevertheless, her story shows that the early church had enough respect for female heroines of the faith that a woman like Thecla would become stamped into legend as a great model of Christian piety.

Entire books have been written to extol the amazing role of women in church history.[4] Their remarkable enterprise and influence caused fourth-century pagan philosopher Libanius to exclaim, "God! What women these Christians have!"[5]

Yet these tributes to Christian women do little to resolve the concerns of those who see the Bible as grotesquely biased toward masculinity. Men undoubtedly played a large role in God's story of redemption. The patriarchs (Abraham, Isaac, Jacob) were all male. The monarchs (David, Solomon, etc.) were all male. The twelve apostles were all male. Noah, Joseph, Moses, Joshua, Samuel, Elijah, Elisha, Daniel, Jonah, Ezra, Nehemiah, Paul, Peter, John...all male. Every identifiable author of Scripture is male. For the typical twenty-first-century reader, a striking amount of testosterone permeates the Bible.

God self-identifies in the Bible as masculine. This alone raises challenges for those who believe God ought not to align with either gender but remain an *it* instead of a *he*. Many who speak of God these days try very hard to adopt gender-neutral terms, but the Bible won't fit that mold. God is described as a father, not a mother. He came to earth as a man, not a woman. He reigns as king, not as queen. These are not small issues. How is a woman to relate to the Bible's message if it seems so oblivious to the fact that half of humanity is not male?

To make matters even worse, a number of Bible passages seem to devalue women and strip them of power. In the book of Genesis, God made Adam first and then made Eve as his "helper" (Genesis 2:18). Paul refers to this order of creation when he says that women are to remain quiet in the church and must not exercise authority over men (1 Timothy 2:11-14). Then there is Ephesians 5:22, which famously says, "Wives, submit to your own husbands" (ESV). You won't find verses like these displayed proudly on posterboard signs at the next women's rights march!

We recognize this subject will be a sensitive topic for many of you reading this book. The tensions we experience are not just concerns or challenges. They are strong points of hurt and contention, for they deal with subjects that touch the essence of our humanity. Simply put, they're personal. Perhaps you have seen the church demote women as second-rate citizens, claiming the Bible to be on their side. Our worst fear in these cases would be that this claim might be correct. In this chapter, we hope to show otherwise. We will give you good reasons to see that the seemingly anti-women sentiment of Scripture is an illusion. A careful understanding of the Bible reveals a good God who deeply values women and gives them a role in society as respectable as that of men.

If you have been hurt by the mishandling of the Bible as a weapon to denigrate women, then we pray this chapter will help you to see Scripture no longer as the source of hurt, but the source of empowerment and healing.

Women in Bible Times

To understand the ways in which the Bible speaks to women, we must put ourselves into the world of the Bible. Almost everyone agrees that the state of equality among women, though not perfect, is much better in most cultures today than it was several thousand years ago. In the biblical context, which mostly includes the Greek, Roman, and Jewish cultures, women were often confined to work at home cleaning, sewing, preparing food, and raising children. Marriages were arranged for them at a very young age.[6] Their testimony was generally distrusted and carried no legal weight.[7] Roles of leadership in society for women were rare. There were restrictions preventing women from having equal participation in religious worship. If you go back far enough in time, you will see very few rights afforded to women and indications that they were seen as the property of their fathers or husbands.[8] Concerning women in ancient Greek culture, Catherine Kroeger writes:

> The Greek woman was thought to have less virtue than a man and to be devoid of moral conscience. Since women could not be trusted to make responsible choices, they might be compelled to remain within their own homes. While certain philosophers propounded a far more enlightened view of women, restrictive customs were the norm in many households. In some, women neither slept nor ate nor discoursed

with the men. The women's quarters were said to be hotbeds of dissension and strife. Literary evidence suggests that sequestered Greek women tended to be depressed, bitter and malicious.[9]

Concerning Jewish life, Dorothy Patterson notes that "the Jewish attitude toward women expressed outside the canon of Scripture at times was discriminatory and demeaning. Many rabbis would not speak to women or teach them."[10]

Needless to say, life was not easy for women back then. Their general disregard is reflected quite sharply in a second-century gnostic text known as the *Gospel of Thomas*. According to saying 114 (Blatz translation): "Simon Peter said to them: Let Mariham go out from among us, for women are not worthy of the life. Jesus said: Look, I will lead her that I may make her male, in order that she too may become a living spirit resembling you males. For every woman who makes herself male will enter into the kingdom of heaven." Commentators point out that the text is not actually saying Jesus will convert women into men. He is simply using women and men as an analogy between lower and higher forms of life.[11] Of course, this explanation does not improve the text's assessment of women. This apocryphal writing differs radically from Jesus's treatment of women in the four Gospels of the New Testament, which have historical grounds for authenticity that are utterly lacking in the *Gospel of Thomas*. For this and many other reasons, Christians do not accept the *Gospel of Thomas* as inspired by God or belonging in the Bible.

The role of women in society as it existed in Bible times affected the way in which Scripture was written. It was written by males because males were more privileged to be educated into literacy.[12] It tells stories of God picking out (mostly) males for leadership because males were the ones whose leadership would be followed. So the Bible's disproportionately high volume of masculinity does not show us a God who favors men over women, but a God who is telling his story in a culture that, unfortunately, did not place females in high regard.

Many people think that despite the biblical upgrades to the status of women, their role in Scripture is little better than that of the cultures from which the Bible emerged. In the following sections, we will address some of the most troubling of these passages.

Woman as Man's Helper?

> The LORD God said, "It is not good for the man to be alone. I will make a helper who is just right for him" (Genesis 2:18).

I (Matthew) still remember when someone wrote to the Josh McDowell Ministry simply to ask, "What is my purpose in life?" To understand our purpose is to understand what we were created for. Cars are created to transport people. Spiderwebs are created to bring in lunch for hungry arachnids. Women are created...*to serve men?*

This verse, Genesis 2:18, which tells us why God created woman, has often been used by anti-Bible feminists to show that God is sexist. But we must not jump to hasty conclusions here. To be a helper does not necessarily imply a lower status or even a hierarchy of any kind. Members of a team help each other. In the first telling of the creation account in Genesis 1, we see God instructing Adam and Eve together to "be fruitful and multiply. Fill the earth and govern it. Reign over the fish in the sea, the birds in the sky, and all animals that scurry along the ground"

(Genesis 1:28). This creation mandate implies some context for the woman being made as a "helper"—not as a sidekick or secretary doing the grunt work, but as a unified team member who contributes vitally toward a common purpose in God's plan for humanity. The man and woman are to be the helpers of each other.

We can take this even further. The Hebrew word for "helper" in Genesis 2:18 is *ezer*. This word shows up sixteen times in the Old Testament text. Ten of these occurrences refer to *God* as being the helper.[13] For instance, in Hosea 13:9, God calls himself the only helper (ezer) of Israel. To anyone who accuses God of being sexist because he created the woman as a helper to the man, we hasten to say that God proudly bears that same title himself!

Some may find it demeaning that the woman was created second, as if making her an inferior off-brand of the man. But one could as easily argue that the woman was created second because God looked at the man and thought he needed to try again! When you consider the order of the creation in Genesis, you find that life begins with the lower orders and proceeds day by day to the higher orders, beginning with sea creatures, reptiles, birds, mammals, and finally culminating in humans. You could argue that woman, as the last being made, stood at the pinnacle of creation. We must not read too much into the order of creation either way. Order does not imply status or value.

Are Wives to Submit to Their Husbands?

Wives, submit yourselves to your own husbands as you do to the Lord (Ephesians 5:22 NIV).

Perhaps more than any other Scripture, this passage is used to accuse the Bible of devaluing the woman's status in the marriage relationship. At first glance, it looks like a hard challenge to answer. How can the equality of women be asserted if they are supposed to submit to the will of their husbands? This looks like a textbook example of an archaic marriage model that modern society has fought hard to erase.

The passage was written by Paul, an apostle of Jesus. Sometimes his writing has been used by abusive men to justify demanding obedience from their wives. But was this Paul's intent? Evidently, these men failed to read through the passage in full:

> Wives, submit yourselves to your own husbands as you do to the Lord. For the husband is the head of the wife as Christ is the head of the church, his body, of which he is the Savior. Now as the church submits to Christ, so also wives should submit to their husbands in everything.

> Husbands, love your wives, just as Christ loved the church and gave himself up for her to make her holy, cleansing her by the washing with water through the word, and to present her to himself as a radiant church, without stain or wrinkle or any other blemish, but holy and blameless. In this same way, husbands ought to love their wives as their own bodies. He who loves his wife loves himself. After all, no one ever hated their own body, but they feed and care for their body, just as Christ does the church—for we are members of his body (Ephesians 5:22-30 NIV).

First, notice Paul's vision for marriage goes both ways, with both the husband and the wife cooperating together *for the sake of each other.* Second, notice Paul's instructions to husbands are significantly longer than his instructions to wives. The reason for this is probably because his message to husbands was quite radical in his time, and it took more explanation to drive home his point. Third, notice how this passage places the greatest burden of marriage on the husbands. Husbands are to love their wives "as Christ loved the church and gave himself up for her." Pause and think about that for a moment. How did Christ give himself up for the church?

Romans 5:8 says, "God demonstrates his own love for us in this: While we were still sinners, Christ died for us" (NIV). Jesus died for the church. That was his display of love! So when Paul tells husbands to love their wives as Christ loved the church, he is beckoning husbands to a radical, self-sacrificial display of love. We might summarize Paul's instructions for marriage in four words: Wives, submit. Husbands, die. Who do you suppose has the better deal here? It makes you begin to think that women may be the most cherished beings in all creation.

We began the above explanation of mutual submission of husbands and wives with Ephesians 5:22 because of the controversy this passage generates with its emphasis on the submission of wives. We believe, however, that the preceding verse, Ephesians 5:21, summarizes the whole of Paul's intent in writing these instructions: "Submit *to one another* out of reverence for Christ" (NIV, emphasis ours). For wives, this means submitting to your husbands as to the Lord. For husbands, it means sacrificing yourself for your wife. For both, it means submitting in love to each other.

There is debate within the church as to how Paul's instructions are supposed to apply in practical settings. Some say the instructions convey the concept of two distinct roles. Others say they convey the same role of mutual submission in two different ways. Regardless, we simply wish to point out that both viewpoints picture a functional marriage powered by love for the sake of the other. Don't you think our society would be in a much better place if husbands and wives took these instructions from Paul more seriously?

Are Women to Be Silent in Church?

> Women should be silent during the church meetings. It is not proper for them to speak. They should be submissive, just as the law says. If they have any questions, they should ask their husbands at home, for it is improper for women to speak in church meetings (1 Corinthians 14:34-35).

This is one of the most puzzling passages in Paul's writings. A first-impression reading seems to imply that women were instructed to remain totally silent during the entire church service. Most interpreters, however, argue the restriction is not what it appears to be. We don't try to qualify this passage because we want a meaning that is easier to swallow. We *do* want greater freedom for women in church, but we must be as unbiased as possible when interpreting Scripture. We find these verses puzzling because earlier in this same letter, Paul had already given instructions concerning proper decorum for women when they prayed or prophesied in the church (1 Corinthians 11:5). This justifies issuing a search warrant to investigate the passage seeming to require total silence. If it is acceptable for women to pray or prophesy in church, then the prohibition against their speaking must mean something different than what it appears to say. Here are a few options that have been considered:

- One suggestion is that women and men sat in separate sections of the church, and it's possible that in the Corinthian church, women kept asking questions to their husbands across the room. This would have created a noisy and distracting environment, so Paul was telling these wives to hold their questions until later.

- A second suggestion is that Paul gave the prohibition to prevent a specific kind of question-asking that was employed as a method of teaching. In Bible times, a teacher would often teach by asking questions, and Paul was instructing women not to assume that teaching role.

- Another suggestion is that this prohibition relates specifically to the preceding section of Scripture regarding the interpretation of prophecies. Perhaps Paul limited this role to men.

- Others suggest Paul's statement on women keeping silent was actually a quotation he was using to explain what the Corinthians were saying about women. Paul brought up the issue in order to rebuke the statement in verse 36. (Biblical Greek did not use quotation marks, so Bible translators must use contextual clues to determine when something is to be put in quotation marks.)

We share these suggestions not in an attempt to resolve the issue but to show that we must be careful about interpreting 1 Corinthians 14:34-35 based on its surface value. We should not be hasty to use this passage as a proof text that Paul and the Bible have an anti-woman bias.

Are Women Prohibited from Teaching?

> Women should learn quietly and submissively. I do
> not let women teach men or have authority over
> them. Let them listen quietly (1 Timothy 2:11-12).

The letter of 1 Timothy contains Paul's instruction to a young man concerning his responsibilities as a pastor to God's people. His instruction for women to "learn quietly" cannot mean they must never speak. The use of "quietly" here should probably be understood in the sense of peacefully, in good order, and with tranquility. That's how the term is used in verse 2 of the same chapter. Certainly, such behavior would also be expected of men, though in this case, Paul felt a need to address women.

This passage has been used to show that Paul had different roles in mind for men and women within the church, and one of those distinctions has to do with authority and teaching. Looking back, we see a similar model in Leviticus, where all priests were male. Looking forward, we see Paul spelling out the qualifications for church overseers, and the entire section uses masculine pronouns to describe them and includes the mandate for them to be "the husband of one wife" (1 Timothy 3:2 ESV).

Despite the apparent distinction between the roles of men and women in the church, some Christian commentators have argued that this understanding of these verses is misguided or limited to a particular context or situation. This is another debated issue within the church that we will not attempt to solve within our limited space. But for the sake of argument, let's assume a straightforward reading—that in the church, women are not allowed to teach or exercise authority over men. If this is true, does it mean the Bible is oppressively limiting the rights of women?

A couple points deserve clarification. First, as we will see later in this chapter, some women in the Bible held positions of leadership, at least one of which involved teaching. So, however we understand this prohibition, it cannot be applied to all forms of teaching in all times and in all places. This is confirmed by theologian Robert Saucy, who researched Paul's meaning behind "teaching" in 1 Timothy and identified how the meaning is limited in certain ways.[14]

Second, the type of ministry that *is* allowed for women is no less important than the type of ministry that is prohibited. As we will see, women would sometimes function as prophets of God both in the Old and New Testaments, and these have historically been extremely important roles in the life of God's people. Because Paul never prohibited women from teaching children, many churches (even the very conservative ones) have women teaching kids' church in Sunday school. Would we say these children are less important than the adults across the hallway? Would we say the teacher's influence among these children is less impactful than the preacher's influence behind the pulpit? Probably not. (We would also add that theologians continue to debate the scope of Paul's statement on women teaching men.)

Do Men Have Higher Status and Authority?

> There is one thing I want you to know: The head of every man is Christ, the head of woman is man, and the head of Christ is God...For the first man didn't come from woman, but the first woman came from man. And man was not made for woman, but woman was made for man (1 Corinthians 11:3, 8-9).

Our previous section addressed the issues raised concerning women teachers in 1 Timothy 2:11-12. In that same passage, Paul prohibited women from exercising authority over men. His logic behind this prohibition is expanded here in 1 Corinthians 11, a passage considered by many commentators to be one of the most difficult to understand in the New Testament. The immediate context is the issue of head coverings, which leads Paul to make a few challenging statements about female roles and authority. Without venturing too deeply into the weeds, we offer the following perspective on this passage to help the concerned reader.

In verse 1, Paul pictures a ladder of authority with Christ at the top rung, man on the next below Christ, and woman below man. At the root of the controversy is the fact that our world tends to take higher authority to mean higher status, importance, and value. But a closer look at the passage clearly refutes this idea. Yes, the head of Christ is God, and Christ submits to the will of the Father,[15] but this does not mean Jesus is less than the Father.[16] By the same reasoning, woman, though being under authority, is not less than the man. Although Paul affirms man was created first, he circles back to remind his readers that every man since then came from a woman (1 Corinthians 11:12). He knows how easily his language could lead the males in his audience to think themselves superior, so he insists that men need women as much as women need men (1 Corinthians 11:11). Their mutual dependence and equal value is solidly affirmed.

In terms of status, Galatians 3:28 (ESV) could not be any clearer: "There is neither Jew nor Greek, there is neither slave nor free, *there is no male and female,* for you are all one in Christ Jesus" (emphasis ours). Paul is not erasing distinctions, but he is erasing the dividing line. All people who place their faith in

Christ are included, no matter the distinction. Whether men and women have equal status and equal roles, or whether they have equal status and different roles—either way, they have equal status! Practically every Christian viewpoint is unified by this belief. As far as we are concerned, there is no valid tradition of Christian thought that says otherwise.

Moreover—and this is key—the Bible does not view authority as a position of dominance. Quite the contrary, it is a position of service and sacrificial love. This position was modeled by Jesus to his disciples in John 13:

> Jesus knew that the Father had given him authority over everything and that he had come from God and would return to God. So he got up from the table, took off his robe, wrapped a towel around his waist, and poured water into a basin. Then he began to wash the disciples' feet, drying them with the towel he had around him. When Jesus came to Simon Peter, Peter said to him, "Lord, are you going to wash my feet?" Jesus replied, "You don't understand now what I am doing, but someday you will." "No," Peter protested, "you will never ever wash my feet!" (John 13:3-8).

Jesus was the acknowledged leader and teacher of his disciples. More than that, he was God incarnate, who had authority over everything. Knowing this, he took on what is considered the lowliest of roles in biblical times: that of washing another's feet. Peter could not understand why Jesus would perform such a lowly task, and we may feel likewise. But this kind of servant-hood is the essence of true leadership, and the church was never meant to operate in any other way. Jesus delivered a similar message in Matthew 20:25-28 (ESV): "You know that the rulers of the Gentiles lord it over them, and their great ones exercise authority over them. It shall not be so among you. But whoever would be great among you must be your servant, and whoever would be first among you must be your slave, even as the Son of Man came not to be served but to serve, and to give his life as a ransom for many."

Any position of authority in the church is to look like Jesus. Paul understood this with his own apostleship. Although he was an appointed apostle of Christ who used his authority to teach and to correct, he knew his position was a place of service and humility, one for which he would have to give an account before God. He wrote, "This is how one should regard us, as servants of Christ and stewards of the mysteries of God" (1 Corinthians 4:1). In light of this, we might say that Paul's distinctions between men and women were actually distinctions delineating how men and women are to serve one another. The distinctions have nothing to do with value or worth or status.

Paul's writings on teaching and authority as they pertain to women certainly challenge us today. We have to understand theology holistically, and this includes the irrefutable affirmation that both men and women have equal value, dignity, and worth as creatures made and loved by God. In light of this truth, some have sought to reinterpret Paul's instructions on teaching and authority to mean something other than hard-and-fast rules differentiating the roles of men and women. But even if we take it that men are to hold authoritative roles and women are not, a proper understanding of the biblical worldview shows that women are equally respected citizens of the kingdom of God. After all, the greater authority a man has over a woman, the more the man must serve and honor her.

Why All the Masculine Words?

Much of the language in the Bible can make it seem that women are left out of the conversation. Masculine terms and pronouns are the norm, and exceptions are few.

For example, the Greek word *adelphoi* ("brothers") is used to address Christians more than 100 times in the New Testament. But this word can be gender-neutral when addressed to a mixed crowd.[17] It would be similar to us addressing a mixed crowd using the word *guys*, except the word *adephoi* expresses a deeper sense of love. Likewise, the Greek word *anthrōpos* could mean "man" or be used more generically for a group of people or for humankind.[18] Newer Bible translations tend to be more sensitive to the word's generic nature and render it accordingly.

The Bible speaks of Christians being adopted as sons of God, but never as daughters. For example, Paul says in Galatians 3:26, "In Christ Jesus you are all sons of God, through faith" (ESV). Some contemporary translations say that we are adopted as "children" of God even though Paul uses the word *huios* ("son") rather than *teknon* ("child"). It is probably best to understand Paul's use of *huios* in terms of function rather than form. Sonship implies inheritance, and this is what Paul was getting at in Galatians 3:26. Only two verses later, Paul follows this passage with his famous words, "There is no male and female, for you are all one in Christ Jesus." This would have been good news to women in the church, who may have worried that God's gift of spiritual inheritance would favor only men.

Women might better endure the prevalence of masculine language in the Bible if they remember that the entire church, including men and women, are considered the bride of Christ (2 Corinthians 11:2; Revelation 19:7).

Positive Examples of Women in the Bible

Considering all that we have studied regarding the place of women in Bible times, it might surprise you to see how often a positive, empowering view of females appears in the biblical narrative. Despite the considerable debate within today's churches about the biblical roles of women, one point the church can agree on is that many women in Scripture were strong-willed, bold, and held important positions of ministry and leadership. They prophesied the words of God. They played vital roles in preserving God's people. They served alongside male leaders like Jesus and Paul. Let's look at some of their stories...

Deborah was not only a prophetess, she was also a judge—a ruler of Israel before it had a monarchy. In Deborah's days, Israel had fallen under the oppression of King Jabin, whose army was commanded by Sisera. In Judges 4, we learn Deborah encouraged her general, Barak, to rally an army against Sisera. Barak insisted she join him as he went to war, and she prophesied that his victory would come at the hand of a woman. Sisera fled Barak on foot and hid in the tent of an Israelite woman named Jael, who killed him with a tent spike.

Huldah was a heroine whose story appears in 2 Kings 22. During the reforms of Josiah, king of Judah, the high priest found God's long-lost book of the law. Josiah, recognizing the tragedy of being so long without God's law, sent the high priest, his secretary, and a handful of royal officials to inquire of God what they must do. These men visited the prophetess Huldah for guidance. She must have been a brave woman, for her words to these important officials were not easy pills to swallow.

Ruth was a strong-willed woman from Moab whose story is recorded in a book of the Bible bearing her name. When her husband died, she insisted on remaining with her mother-in-law,

Naomi, a widow whom she faithfully served and supported with love and compassion. The book ends by connecting her as a key figure in the royal lineage of King David (Ruth 4:13-17), ultimately making her an ancestor of Jesus.

Esther, like Ruth, has a book in Scripture bearing her name and dedicated to her story. As a young woman, she was brought to the king of Persia, who admired her beauty and made her queen. During this time, a powerful official named Haman sought to kill all the Jews in Persia. Esther twice risked her life by approaching the king unauthorized to plead for the lives of her people. The king listened. Esther's bravery saved the Persian Jews from annihilation.

Rahab, a Canaanite woman, risked her life because she believed in the God of Israel. She bravely hid the Israelite spies in her home and devised a shrewd plan to get them safely out of the city. Her courage is enshrined in Hebrews 11:31 among the other models of faith in Scripture.

Priscilla and her husband, Aquila, served as important companions to Paul in the formation of the early church. The couple "risked their necks" for Paul's life (Romans 16:4). What's interesting about this missionary duo is that Priscilla is often mentioned first among the two, suggesting that she had a more prominent role as a missionary.[19]

Mary was the mother of Jesus. Luke 1 introduces her story in contrast with Zechariah, a Jewish priest who heard from an angel that God was going to give him a child who would greatly influence the people of Israel. Zechariah failed to trust the angel's message. Mary also heard from an angel that God would give her a child though she was a virgin, and this child would be called Son of the Most High. Unlike Zechariah, she trusted the message, submitted herself as servant to the Lord, and became the means by which God brought Jesus into the world. Imagine that!—the Bible presents the woman Mary with greater honor than a male priest. It's clear Luke is giving a countercultural lesson on where godliness is truly found.

These are some of the heroines in Scripture who tend to get the most attention. But there are many other examples who pay tribute to female bravery or leadership in a male-dominated world.

- Besides Deborah and Huldah, other prophetesses in Scripture include Isaiah's wife (Isaiah 8:3), Miriam (Exodus 15:20), Noadiah (Nehemiah 6:14), and Anna (Luke 2:36).

- God used a woman to punish Abimelech for his evil (Judges 9:53, 56).

- The book of Proverbs personifies wisdom as a woman (1:20) and speaks highly of a mother's teaching (1:8; 6:20; 31:26).

- God rewarded Shiphrah and Puah, two Hebrew midwives, for standing up against Pharaoh of Egypt (Exodus 1:15-21).

- The daughters of Zelophehad boldly asked Moses for the inheritance from their deceased father because he had no sons to carry on the family name. God told Moses to grant their request despite the cultural norm, which was to allot inheritances to men only. Then God codified their case into a law to protect women in similar predicaments (Numbers 27:1-11).

- A number of women traveled with Jesus alongside the apostles and financially supported his ministry (Luke 8:1-3).

- Acts 17:4 tells us that many "leading women" were persuaded by the preaching of Paul and Silas. The author, Luke, probably considered this detail important because of the high level of influence these women would exercise in the church.

- In Romans 16:1-2, Paul commends Phoebe to the Roman church, instructing them to welcome her as a saint and to help her with her requests.

- In Romans 16:7, Paul compliments Junia as a woman "well known to the apostles."

- In 1 Corinthians 11:5, Paul gives instruction for women who were praying or prophesying in the church.

- When Jesus's disciples scattered after his arrest, it was women who stayed with him until the bitter end on the cross (Matthew 27:55-56; Mark 15:40-41), and it was women who become the first witnesses of the resurrected Christ (Matthew 28:1-3; Mark 16:1-7).

All of this shows that there are some extraordinary women featured in the Bible. Their recognition is a testament to God's desire that they would be valued with as much respect as men. Women did not have it easy back then, but they were still given significant parts to play in the story of Scripture. It is truly unprecedented to see such a positive view of women portrayed in a book written thousands of years ago.

God was good to women because he is a good God. It is no wonder then, that Jesus's life is filled with stories of his kind treatment of women and the way he admired their displays of faith. At one point, Jesus's disciples were surprised to find him talking to a woman (John 4:27), but he did much more for them than that! He healed a bleeding woman because of her display of faith (Matthew 9:20-22). He commended the faith of a Canaanite woman for her clever response (Matthew 15:28). He had women followers (Luke 8:1-3). He defended a woman who was scolded for anointing him with costly perfume (Mark 14:3-9). He taught his disciples generosity through the display of a widow's offering (Luke 21:1-4). He taught about prayer through an illustration about a persistent widow (Luke 18:1-8). When Jesus helped a woman to see her own sin and showed her the way of life, she was amazed and ran off to tell everyone in town about him (John 4:1-42).

"Jesus himself was not hostage to the sexism of his day," writes New Testament scholar D.A. Carson.[20] Quite the opposite—he stood up for women and treated them with radical displays of love and acceptance.

By now we hope it's apparent the Bible reflects a highly positive view of women. Their infinite value comes from the same place as that of men. According to Genesis 1:27, God created men and women in his image.[21] While the depth of meaning behind God's image has been pondered for millennia, it is certain that this status which applies to all humanity is high and sacred. No other worldview outside that of the Judeo-Christian religions understands humanity as God's image bearers.

The Story of "Pleasant"

According to *The Eerdmans Bible Dictionary,* "Names carry more value and importance in biblical than in modern usage. Not only may a name identify, but it frequently expresses the essential nature of its bearer; to know the name is to know the person."[22] Hence God changed Abram's name to Abraham, meaning "father of many" (Genesis 17:5), and Jesus changed Simon's name to Peter, meaning "rock" (John 1:42).

Another biblical name that deserves our attention is Naomi, meaning "pleasant." Naomi and her family were from Bethlehem in Judah, but because of a severe famine in the land, they packed up, left their home, and settled in the land of Moab. Then, in a tragic turn of events, Naomi's husband died.

In the following years, Naomi's two sons married women from Moab. But in another tragic turn, both of them died. It is hard to imagine the kind of grief Naomi would have experienced losing her husband and children, leaving her alone in a world where it was very difficult for a woman to survive. So "Pleasant" was left grieving the loss of her family as a vulnerable, childless widow in a foreign land. She could offer no future to her two Moabite daughters-in-law. Circumstances could not get any more difficult for her.

With nowhere else to go, Naomi returned to her homeland. The people recognized her and excitedly asked, "Is that Naomi?" But the sound of that name burned her ears in terrible irony. "'Don't call me Naomi,' she responded. 'Instead, call me Mara ["bitter"], for the Almighty has made life very bitter for me. I went away full, but the LORD has brought me home empty. Why call me Naomi when the LORD has caused me to suffer and the Almighty has sent such tragedy upon me?'" (Ruth 1:20-21).

This poor widow's response captures the feeling of many women who believe God is against them. In this chapter, we have explored the major issues that have led some to believe certain tragic lies. The truth is that all women are beautiful and precious in God's eyes and fully included in the life of Christ. Unfortunately, an unhealthy church or a misunderstanding of Scripture has made this difficult for some women to believe. But God is a God who uses hardship to show his kindness. In the case of Naomi, through a marvelous set of serendipitous circumstances, God found a suitable and willing husband for her daughter-in-law, Ruth. Together, they bore a grandson to Naomi. Her story concludes with these words:

> The women of the town said to Naomi, "Praise the LORD, who has now provided a redeemer for your family! May this child be famous in Israel. May he restore your youth and care for you in your old age. For he is the son of your daughter-in-law who loves you and has been better to you than seven sons!" Naomi took the baby and cuddled him to her breast. And she cared for him as if he were her own. The neighbor women said, "Now at last Naomi has a son again!" And they named him Obed. He became the father of Jesse and the grandfather of David (Ruth 4:14-17).

What a remarkable ending! It reveals the purpose of this story's inclusion in the Bible. It shines light on a good God who blossomed new life into a widow whose spirit had died with the rest of her family. Though Naomi wished to be called "bitter," thinking God was against her, God actually blessed her in ways she never imagined. Consequently, Naomi's suggested name change did not even last into the next verse![23] Her life and heritage were preserved through the gift of a son, a predecessor of the royal line of King David and of Christ himself.[24] God was never the cause of Naomi being bitter. He isn't like that. As it turned out, Naomi learned through her story that some names just don't stick.

9

Turning Up the Heat on Eternal Destiny

I can indeed hardly see how anyone ought to wish
Christianity to be true; for if so the plain language of
the text seems to show that the men who
do not believe, and this would include my Father,
Brother and almost all my best friends,
will be everlastingly punished.
And this is a damnable doctrine.[1]

—CHARLES DARWIN

When the only remedy for human sin is rejected and all
appeals of a loving, seeking God for the reconciliation
of rebellious sinners are refused, there is no other
course of action which God himself can pursue but to
leave the sinner to his self-chosen destiny.[2]

—RALPH POWELL

Back in 2011, former pastor Rob Bell published his book *Love Wins*, which sought to challenge the Bible's teaching on the existence of hell. Bell's book sparked a controversy in the church and became about as fiery as the topic itself. Later that year, Francis Chan and Preston Sprinkle released their own book, *Erasing Hell*, which challenged Bell's position and presented a biblical case for the reality of hell. As a young, evangelical college student, I (Matthew) was excited to study this topic and see if Chan and Sprinkle's ideas would counter Bell's. My perception changed after I cracked open their book and read the first eleven words of the introduction: "If you are excited to read this book, you have issues."[3]

Chan and Sprinkle's opening statement may not reflect the best marketing strategy, but they call out what many Christians tend to ignore—that hell is a deeply sobering reality for Christians to deal with. In the traditional view, hell is a place of eternal, conscious punishment for anyone who fails to receive Jesus for the forgiveness of their sins. We cannot take this doctrine lightly.

Of everything else that atheists and skeptics use to argue against the goodness of God, hell makes them look like child's play. How could we imagine that our own friends and family might end up there, suffering every minute of every hour of every day of every year, on and on for eternity, because they never believed in the saving power of Jesus? For many, the mere thought of this is paralyzing or even traumatizing. The doctrine of hell makes it easy to see why people become disillusioned with God as a vindictive torturer whose volume of cruelty defies language.

Many in the church have denied the reality of hell or reimagined it in a way easier for them to accept. Although these alternative views of hell are mistaken, they are, in a sense, the "right" kind of mistakes. These views find their strength in a theological conviction that God is good, and any doctrine that claims otherwise cannot stand. However, the problem does not lie in the traditional view of hell (eternal, conscious punishment), but in false caricatures of the traditional view. By peeling away false perceptions of hell, we will be ready to understand how it fits into the biblical picture along with the goodness of God. By the end of this chapter, we hope to show that the traditional view of hell is actually the best option for a good God to offer those who choose to reject his plan of salvation.

Outside the City

Hell is often characterized as an underground torture chamber, especially by medieval paintings of naked men and women engulfed in flames while Satan and his demon slave drivers torture them with pitchforks. These paintings reflect only the inflamed imagination of artists and show us nothing of what hell is actually like. For starters, Satan and his demons are not running the place; they will be punished in hell just like anyone else.[4] More to our point, hell is not to be understood primarily by what it is or where it is, but where it isn't.

Although the word *hell* never shows up in the Old Testament,[5] the concept certainly does. Daniel speaks of the end times as a day when all the dead are raised out of Sheol (a general term for "grave" or "place of the dead") and assigned their eternal destinies: "Many of those whose bodies lie dead and buried will rise up, some to everlasting life and some to shame and everlasting disgrace" (Daniel 12:2). Isaiah provides further insight, saying that people who experience everlasting life will come to worship God and "go out" to see all the dead bodies of those who rebelled against God (Isaiah 66:22-24). It is a place where "the worms that devour them will never die, and the fire that burns them will never go out" (verse 24).

In Revelation 20, Jesus returns as the king of the world and reigns for 1,000 years. Then the sea, death, and Hades give up their dead. In other words, Sheol is emptied out, and all the dead are resurrected. Death and Hades are thrown into the "lake of fire," signaling the ultimate end of death and Sheol. There is a "book of life" containing names, and anyone not listed in that book is thrown into the lake of fire.

Revelation 21 opens to a new heaven and new earth. God's city, the New Jerusalem, comes down from heaven like a beautifully adorned bride being presented to her husband. Then a heavenly voice proclaims that God has made his dwelling among the people. Finally, abundant life in the presence of God is fully and permanently realized. What a moment! But only those whose names are written in the book of life (the ones not already thrown in the lake of fire) will enter the city.

Notice that the ultimate end for unsaved humanity is characterized by being *outside*, according to Isaiah and Revelation. This matches the teaching of Jesus. The word he often used that is translated "hell" in the Greek New Testament was *Gehenna*. Although *Gehenna* was clearly used to indicate the place of final judgment for unbelievers, it was also a physical place just outside the city of Jerusalem. The land had been used for acts of tremendous evil. It was the place where Israel's idolatrous kings sacrificed their sons to Moloch and the Babylonians slaughtered the Jews in their siege of Jerusalem (Jeremiah 19:1-13). Later it served as a dumping ground where garbage and the dead bodies of criminals were burned.[6] Gehenna was an appropriate illustration for hell because there was rebellion against God, there was fire, and it sat *outside the city of Jerusalem*.

Hell is banishment. It is what happens when you are kicked out of the party. The New Jerusalem—God's heavenly city—is the place where God dwells, but hell is outside the city. As we mentioned in chapter 7, the Garden of Eden and the tabernacle were about life and the presence of God. Hell is precisely *not that*. It is death and separation from relationship with God. This is what makes hell so horrible.

But What About the Fire?

At this point, you may wonder if we are blowing smoke, conjuring up a picture of hell that is easier to stomach while avoiding the fact that hell is characterized by the torment of fire. Minimizing the horror of hell is not our intention. As we pointed out earlier, hell is not merely a neutral zone outside God's city; it is called a place or a lake of fire.[7] However, fire is not the only descriptor Scripture provides for hell. It is also a place of "darkness" (Matthew 8:12; 2 Peter 2:17). It is a place where "the worms that devour them will never die" (Isaiah 66:24; see also Mark 9:48). It is the "second death" (Revelation 20:14-15). It is a place that destroys (Matthew 10:28), a place of "everlasting destruction" (2 Thessalonians 1:9). The fact that we have all these different descriptors suggests that hell is presented to us not literally but figuratively from multiple angles. With literal fire, there would be light, but hell is a place of darkness.

We suggest the lake of fire in Revelation should be taken figuratively as well. In support of this view, notice that "death" and Hades (i.e., Sheol, the realm of the dead) are also thrown into the lake of fire (Revelation 20:14). How could death or a realm be literally thrown into a lake? Figurative language is common in Revelation and typical of its genre of literature. The fiery lake signals ultimate destruction and judgment.

A figurative approach to hellfire is probably the most common view among evangelical scholars today. There is no rule within the boundaries of conservative theology that demands a literal interpretation of fire.[8] Rather than suggesting a physical experience of burning alive, hell is the experience of complete and utter separation from the presence of God. It is, as we have already stated, the experience of being cast out from the source of all life and goodness. The pain is both spiritual and emotional. According to theologian J.I. Packer, "The concept [of hell] is formed by systematically negating every element in the experience of God's goodness as believers know it through grace and as all mankind knows it through kindly providences (Acts 14:16-17; Ps. 104:10-30; Rom. 2:4)."[9] To wonder how the absence of God could be so horrible only goes to show how much we take for granted God's sustaining of life on earth. To lose this universal grace would be experientially violent, like a fish suddenly pulled out of water, unaware that the water had been sustaining its life the whole time.

We would be wrong to think that a nonliteral interpretation of fire softens the intensity of hell. The Bible uses the term "fire" because fire is a fitting description of hell's effect. The torment of hell is as extreme as the pain of fire, but the fact that it is figurative enables us to understand that hell is not intended for *torture*. God did not light the fire; it comes from within the doomed person. The idea of God inflicting torture presents a false caricature of hell that must be corrected. Hell is torment but not torture. Or, as philosopher J.P. Moreland put it, "Hell *is* punishment—but it's not punish*ing*."[10]

We already understand the pain of hell to some extent through our own broken relationships on earth. Rejection, isolation, and loneliness are painful because we were made for relationship with one another. When these relationships are ruptured, the emotional torment can be extremely intense. Figurative burning in hell is no joke. In fact, it is a sobering reality that some people will physically burn themselves as an attempt to distract them-selves from the weight of emotional pain![11] How much more tormenting must it be to experience total separation from God?

The reason hell is so bad is because God is so good. So good, in fact, that life without God would be hell. The logic of hell in the Bible only makes sense if God is supremely good. As Paul says in 2 Thessalonians 1:9, "They will be punished with eternal destruction, forever separated from the Lord and from his glorious power."

By Human Hands

Modern people often imagine God puts us on earth to "do the right stuff" before our time runs out lest we are suddenly plunged into eternal darkness. We may even visualize the souls of hell crying to God for mercy, but God says, "Too late! You had your chance. Now you will suffer my wrath." However, when we understand that the pain of hell is relational separation from God, we begin to recognize that hell does not initiate a sudden, unexpected tormenting of surprised victims. Hell is the final result of a trajectory on which people have willingly traveled all their lives. According to 2 Peter 2:17-22, the unsaved are already engaged with the essence of hell, sinking deeper and deeper into it. This trajectory of hell is further supported by the fact that hellfire is associated with people even while they are still alive on earth. Jude 23 speaks of saving others "by snatching them out of the fire" (ESV). Similarly, James 3:6 says that the tongue, left unchecked, sets the entire course of life on fire, and is itself set on fire by hell. In none of these passages is God inflicting people with the pain of hell. They have chosen to go that direction themselves. The fires of hell are lit by human hands. According to theologian J.I. Packer,

> Scripture sees hell as self-chosen; those in hell will realize that they sentenced themselves to it by loving darkness rather than light, choosing not to have their Creator as their Lord, preferring self-indulgent sin

to self-denying righteousness, and (if they encountered the gospel) rejecting Jesus rather than coming to him (John 3:18-21; Rom. 1:18, 24, 26, 28, 32; 2:8; 2 Thess. 2:9-11). General revelation confronts all mankind with this issue, and from this standpoint hell appears as God's gesture of respect for human choice. All receive what they actually chose, either to be with God forever, worshiping him, or without God forever, worshiping themselves. Those who are in hell will know not only that for their doings they deserve it but also that in their hearts they chose it.[12]

"Wait a minute," you say. "Is hell judgment from God, or is hell something we choose ourselves?" It's both. With hell, it seems to be that God's judgment involves giving people over to their desires, allowing their own foolish actions to take their course. Similarly, in Romans 1:18, Paul says that "God shows his anger from heaven against all sinful, wicked people who suppress the truth by their wickedness." How? "God abandoned them to do whatever shameful things their hearts desired" (Romans 1:24).

Why would anyone in his or her right mind choose hell? Consider how often people commit self-harm every time they push others away, isolate themselves on social media, shoot up with heroin, or bury themselves with unnecessary debt. Often such people are unwilling to change even if they see their own problems and are offered a solution. Humans have an amazing capacity for self-destruction, being miserable and yet intent on retaining their misery. Our modes of self-destruction are easily hidden under the borrowed pleasure they bring, like the high from drugs, the perception of superiority in pushing others away, the feeling of security in owning things, or the sensation of illicit sex. If the punishment of hell is the full effect of our self-destructive habits contrary to God's purpose, it is not hard to imagine why many choose it.

"Get me out of here!"

One of the most devastating natural disasters to hit the United States in recent times was Hurricane Katrina. This Category 5 storm pummeled New Orleans and the surrounding areas, claiming more than 1,800 lives. Prior to the storm, many residents chose not to evacuate, thinking their property could handle it. But as the floodwaters violently surged, they were immediately crushed with fear and regret. According to one survivor, "People was [sic] yelling, banging on the roofs of houses from the inside. They'd climbed up to get away from the water and got themselves stuck in their attics with no way to break out...But here it was a-flooding, and that nasty water was drowning folks like rats in they [sic] own houses."[13]

Those who chose to wait out the storm never chose to drown or become stranded on their roofs for days on end. Had they known the severe consequences of their choices, they would have fled their city like most others did. Could the same be said about eternity? Sure, people may choose separation from God, but are they really choosing hell? If they could only understand what the experience of hell is like, wouldn't they immediately decide against it? Upon actually experiencing hell, wouldn't they immediately change their mind and want out?

In Luke 16, Jesus tells the story of a rich man who lived luxuriously while a poor man named Lazarus sat helpless at his gate. Both men died. The rich man went to a place of torment, and Lazarus went to heaven to be by Abraham's side. It's clear the rich man is not enjoying himself, but look at how the story unfolds...

The rich man shouted, "Father Abraham, have some pity! Send Lazarus over here to dip the tip of his finger in water and cool my tongue. I am in anguish in these flames."

But Abraham said to him, "Son, remember that during your lifetime you had everything you wanted, and Lazarus had nothing. So now he is here being comforted, and you are in anguish. And besides, there is a great chasm separating us. No one can cross over to you from here, and no one can cross over to us from there."

Then the rich man said, "Please, Father Abraham, at least send him to my father's home. For I have five brothers, and I want him to warn them so they don't end up in this place of torment."

But Abraham said, "Moses and the prophets have warned them. Your brothers can read what they wrote."

The rich man replied, "No, Father Abraham! But if someone is sent to them from the dead, then they will repent of their sins and turn to God."

But Abraham said, "If they won't listen to Moses and the prophets, they won't be persuaded even if someone rises from the dead" (Luke 16:24-31).

The rich man asks Abraham to send Lazarus down from heaven to help him find relief in the fires of torment. But notice what the rich man *doesn't* ask. He never asks Abraham to send him up to heaven. If he was bold enough to ask Lazarus to come down, wouldn't he have rather asked to come up? First, the rich man probably realized that his predicament was deserved. He never cried unfair play. Second, as many commentators point out, the rich man doesn't appear to have a change of heart, even after biting the bullet of his actions. All these years, Lazarus sat begging at the gate while the rich man indulged in the pleasures of life, and now all that the rich man thinks about is for Lazarus to come down and serve him or to be his messenger boy. Even though the rich man recognizes that his brothers would be better off in heaven, his own disposition is still bent away from God. He made his choice and was sticking to it. He wanted to remain king of his own life, even if it meant being a king in hell. As Ralph Powell states in the *Baker Encyclopedia of the Bible*, "There is no indication anywhere in Scripture that lost sinners in hell are capable of repentance and faith."[14]

In some ways, it is hard to imagine how someone experiencing the fire of hell would choose to continue wallowing in such torment. But in other ways, it really isn't. Those who are in a place without God, a place where people are given over to their own direction in life toward sin, will experience the full force of sin's power. They will experience anger, stubbornness, grumbling, regret, and all kinds of negative emotions in which they distance themselves further and further from others. Consider this: What happens when you tell a stubborn person to stop being stubborn? What happens when you tell an angry person to stop being angry? It doesn't work! Even though they are miserable, they cling to their misery rather than release their anger by forgiving the offender. As C.S. Lewis put it, "There is always something they insist on keeping even at the price of misery."[15]

People tend to be stubborn in their ways. What makes us think they would suddenly have a change of heart in a place where there is nothing to curb the excesses of the self?

What About Those Who Have Never Heard?

We have argued that people willingly choose hell because they willingly choose to separate themselves from God in order to maintain their independence. But what about the billions who have never heard of Jesus or the salvation he offers? Are they doomed to hell simply because they were born in a Muslim or Hindu or Buddhist culture?

It's true that some people are born in strong Christian environments, while others are not. Because of this, we can easily assume they have an unfair advantage. But the Bible does not give the impression you need to be born in a Christian home to have a fair shot at salvation. All it says is that you have to be born. In chapter 2 of this book, we showed that God's judgment does not come without warning. Romans 1:18-20 teaches that God's presence and power are clearly displayed in nature, and people who ignore or reject these evidences are without excuse.

Consider what Paul said in Acts 17:26-27 (NIV): "From one man [God] made all the nations, that they should inhabit the whole earth; and he marked out their appointed times in history and the boundaries of their lands. God did this so that they would seek him and perhaps reach out for him and find him, though he is not far from any one of us." This passage suggests that God ordained everyone to be born in the most ideal situation possible for him. Because God knows us intimately even before we are born,[16] he is able to assign us to a time and place where we are most likely to find salvation in him. For some, this means being born in a Christian environment. For others, it does not.

I (Josh) was one of those others. Growing up in a broken family, I learned to hate God. My hatred for God led me on a quest to intellectually disprove Christianity. But after a long investigation, I came to realize that the Christian message was true. This opened my heart to understand God's love for me and receive his forgiveness. As it turned out, God used my unique personality and circumstances to lead me to himself. Had I grown up in a different environment, even a Christian one, I might never have chosen to receive Jesus.

There is hope of finding salvation in Christ even for those who have never been told about Jesus. For instance, many former Muslims report becoming a Christian after Jesus revealed himself to them in a dream.[17] Often, these dreams are taken seriously because of the culture they grew up in—the culture where God placed them.

One may object that God has not given us enough evidence to believe in him. I (Josh) have written many books to the contrary, showing that God has given us overwhelming evidence to support belief. It has been humbling to see him use my resources such as *More Than a Carpenter* and *Evidence That Demands a Verdict* to convince many thousands around the world that Jesus is alive.

Lack of evidence is not the issue here; it's the suppression of evidence in our heart. Look back to the story of the rich man and Lazarus. The rich man wanted Abraham to send Lazarus to warn his brothers, but Abraham insisted that if they didn't listen to Moses and the prophets, they wouldn't believe even if someone rose from the dead. Abraham's statement was not mere theory. Jesus rose from the dead, and yet many of the Jews still did not accept him as their Savior.

God is fair in his judgment, which he renders in accordance with a person's knowledge. In John 15:22, Jesus said, "They would not be guilty if I had not come and spoken to them. But now they have no excuse for their sin." Likewise, in Luke

12:47-48, he said, "A servant who knows what the master wants, but isn't prepared and doesn't carry out those instructions, will be severely punished. But someone who does not know, and then does something wrong, will be punished only lightly. When someone has been given much, much will be required in return; and when someone has been entrusted with much, even more will be required."

This passage helps us to see that God's judgment is weighed against a person's knowledge. Although many people think the judgment of hell is a one-size-fits-all deal, the Bible offers no evidence that hell imposes a uniform experience on all its inhabitants. In fact, there's biblical evidence for different degrees of judgment in hell, just as there may be different degrees of reward in heaven, as suggested by the parable of the talents.[18] According to Powell,

> While the duration of punishment in hell is eternal for all who have chosen that destiny for themselves, there are degrees of punishment proportional to the degrees of guilt of each individual. Only God is able to determine what those degrees are, and he will assign the consequences with perfect justice according to the responsibility of each one. Evidence of such gradations in future punishment is found in Scripture (Mt 11:20-24; Lk 12:47, 48; Rv 20:12, 13; cf. Ez 16:48-61). An obvious comparison is made in these texts between the differing intensities of punishment that are involved in the contrasting privileges, knowledge, and opportunities.[19]

At the end of the day, our job is to trust in God for our own salvation and to proclaim his good news to others. God's job is to judge the world according to his perfect standard of righteousness. We can leave that in his capable hands.

Hell and the Goodness of God

The image of people dying, suddenly being enflamed in agonizing torture—not having the slightest clue as to why or how—and screaming to find escape is not what the Bible teaches about hell. Rather, hell is the final destination of those who walked in its direction all their life. Given what we have discovered, we are now ready to unpack the ways in which God has revealed himself as good through the doctrine of hell.

First, hell is a form of God's protection. Speaking of God's heavenly city, Revelation 21:26-27 says, "All the nations will bring their glory and honor into the city. Nothing evil will be allowed to enter, nor anyone who practices shameful idolatry and dishonesty—but only those whose names are written in the Lamb's Book of Life." Hell exists not because God desires to torture people, but because God desires to keep his heavenly abode pure. Contrary to popular atheist speculation, Christians can appreciate hell not because they want to see everyone else burn, but because they are comforted in knowing that God will keep his house clean from all forms of moral corruption. God can do this because he has designated a place outside the city as a separate repository for corruption.

Second, God honors people's choices either to choose or reject him by designating this place for them outside his city. Many people today say they would rather go to hell than spend eternity worshipping God in heaven. We have no reason to doubt their sincerity. God is prepared to honor their choice if they do not have a change of heart during their lifetime on earth. Once again, C.S. Lewis conveys the idea well: "There are only two kinds of people in the end: those who say to God, 'Thy will be done,' and those to whom God says, in the end, 'Thy will be done.'"[20]

Third, just as God honors human choice, hell shows us that God honors human life. From the very beginning, God made humanity in his own image (Genesis 1:27), with the implication that human life is sacred. So God is committed to honoring human life rather than ending it. Instead of forcing unwilling people into his kingdom or ending their lives forever, God quarantines them to a place where they can live out their own choice.

Fourth, hell reveals that God is both holy and serious about sin. As we stated earlier in the book, we have a built-in sense of justice that says evil ought to be punished. Without hell, there is no sense of ultimate judgment. Everyone's final destiny would end up being the same—from Hitler to Martin Luther King Jr. But God, a righteous judge, will ensure justice is carried out, including for those who spent their entire lifetime on earth doing evil and getting away with it. Further, the fact that God acts as judge means we can have the confidence to forgive rather than taking matters into our own hands. As Paul said in Romans 12:19: "Dear friends, never take revenge. Leave that to the righteous anger of God." We can do this because God has designated a place outside the city.

Should Hell Disturb Us?

Don't misunderstand us—even though hell helps to reveal the ways in which God is good, we are not saying people should be happy about the reality of this horrible place. In speaking about hell, the skeptics and atheists are right about one thing: Hell *should* disturb us. Their error is in thinking hell should cause us to reject God. We would argue that the reality of hell should drive us toward God, not away from him. Arguably the most famous writing on hell came not from an atheist seeking to dissuade people from belief in God, but from a sermon that propelled one of the largest Christian revivals in American history.[21]

Our reaction to hell should take place on both a personal and corporate level. *Personally*, the reality of hell is meant to drive us to our knees and causes us to repent of our sin before God. Hell was never meant to be a fear tactic to scare us into heaven, but it does provide an eye-opening revelation about the magnitude of our own sin. *Corporately*, hell should lead us to urge others to consider Christ while there is still time for them to change their trajectory and finalize their decision. God does not just tell us about hell; he tells us that we can do something about it.[22]

We find hell disturbing to our conscience because God made us that way. We suspect God did this because the prospect of hell for any human person, in a sense, disturbs him too. As we read in 1 Timothy 2:3-4, "This is good and pleases God our Savior, who wants everyone to be saved and to understand the truth." God's intention for humankind was that people would never choose such a horrible destiny for themselves, forever separated from relationship with him. In fact, Matthew 25:41 says hell was prepared for the devil and his demons. God never desired to send people there.

A Fork in the Road

As our chapter comes to a close, we would do well to remember what we already learned in chapter 1 about sin and the holiness of God. I (Matthew) have often tried to help others understand these things through the following illustration.

Imagine you are walking on a path, and you come to a fork in the road. At that juncture you see two signs posted. The first sign reads, "This way to hell for eternal punishment away from the presence of God." The other sign reads, "This way to heaven for eternal glory and fullness of life in the presence of God."

Which path would you choose?

In this scenario, anyone in his or her right mind would take the path straight to heaven without a second thought. But wait; there is more to the story.

Imagine reaching this fork and seeing God standing there. Suddenly you tremble, your knees buckle, and you fall to the ground overwhelmed by the intense, infinite glory and light that shines forth from God's majestic holiness. The extreme purity of the light exposes to your eyes the extreme darkness, depravity, and wretchedness of the sin that contaminates your soul. In that moment you realize that every sin you ever committed was an affront to this holy God who created you to be like himself. You grovel in guilty agony as you cover your head with your arms and cry out like Isaiah did when he encountered God, "It's all over! I am doomed, for I am a sinful person."[23]

Surely any one of us who experienced this moment without any sense of God's loving grace would be overcome with abject shame, convinced we now faced inevitable ruin and that we deserved it. It's likely God would have no need to send us to hell. I think we would escort ourselves.

Thanks be to God, none of us need to face the doom depicted in this scenario. The essence of the Christian message is that those who place their trust in the saving power of Christ will not experience this moment without any sense of God's amazing grace freely given. On the contrary, we will know it fully. This illustration of the fork in the road does not just show us the hellish nature of our own sin, it also sets us up to understand the beauty of the gospel message. People have condemned the fork that leads to hell as unjust and cruel, forgetting that God leaves it open as a free alternative for all who choose to reject him. Yet despite our sin, he invites us to take the other path—the one paved by his grace, which he has opened and cleared at an enormous cost to himself.

Despite what some people think, the goodness of God shines brightest at the foot of the cross. It is the most profound expression of God's righteous judgment and his relentless love fully realized. It is the story of how God looked down upon the abyss of hell, its jaws of death opened wide to swallow the entirety of sin-contaminated humanity, and he stretched out his hands as if to say, "Over my dead body!"

This will be the subject of our final chapter.

10

Why Would God Kill His Own Son?

After their return from Babylon, the practice of human sacrifice died out among the Jews, but survived as an ideal in one of its break-away sects, which believed that God accepted the torture-sacrifice of an innocent man in exchange for not visiting a worse fate on the rest of humanity. The sect is called Christianity.[1]

—STEVEN PINKER

In two decades of teaching theology, I have had countless students ask me why God doesn't save everybody. Only once did a student come to me and say, "There is something I just can't figure out. Why did God redeem me?"[2]

—R.C. SPROUL

Back in 1963, researchers at Yale University conducted a controversial experiment. Participants were told they would be helping to measure the effectiveness of punishment to stimulate memory. They were given the role of "teachers," and each was taken individually to a room with a "learner." The learner was strapped to a kind of electric chair, and the participant's job was to

issue electric shocks with increasing volts of electricity whenever
the learner failed to remember what he had been taught earlier that
day. Participants were informed that the shocks could be extremely
painful but would not cause permanent damage. The learner exhibited greater and greater distress as the electric shocks increased in
severity, to the point that he was protesting, pounding the wall in
agony, and even lapsed into unconsciousness. Not surprisingly, the
participants of this study would grow very uncomfortable and ask
to end the experiment prematurely. Yet the instructor urged them
to finish the study, all the way through thirty levels of increasing shock intensity. The lowest intensity on the shock machine
was labeled 15 volts under the heading "Slight Shock." The highest intensity was labeled 450 volts, five levels beyond the heading "Danger: Severe Shock," and one level beyond the ominous
"XXX."

The shock machine was fake. The "learner" was just an actor.
The researchers were not testing memory at all. The experiment
was designed to see how obedient the unknowing participants
would be to following instructions that went against their own
conscience. Of the forty participants, who came from a wide
range of occupations and educational levels, more than half
finished the study to the very end.[3]

Nobody on the research team expected results like this. As it
turned out, the same inner tendency that generated destructive
obedience in German Nazi soldiers twenty years prior existed
deep in the hearts of postal clerks, schoolteachers, salespersons,
and engineers in and around New Haven, Connecticut. But it
wasn't just the research team that was surprised. *The participants
were aghast to find this proclivity within themselves.* According to
their report, "In the post-experimental interviews subjects took
pains to point out that they were not sadistic types."[4]

Reflecting on this study, theologian Cornelius Plantinga Jr. confronts us with a question we are forced to reckon with:

> Why? Why would any ordinary person punish an innocent, protesting, screaming, and finally silent stranger in this way? None of the obedient shockers looked like scrofulous monsters. Most gave little outward indication that they were even particularly aggressive, let alone hostile. A number identified themselves as members in good standing of Christian churches. Virtually all of them, when interviewed, stated their opposition, in principle, to hurting innocent people. Yet, what they rejected in principle they did in practice, however distressed they felt about it. They did it because somebody in a laboratory coat told them that they had no choice.[5]

Evidently, the participants discovered something buried deep within themselves, something they didn't like and refused to acknowledge. They discovered what the Bible calls sin.

As a noun, sin is the poison that dissolves the human heart, corrupts our world, and alienates humans from God and from each other. As a verb, sin is the dispensing of this poison through our thoughts, attitudes, and actions. Because of sin, we are separated from God and trapped on a one-way road to hell. All of us have drunk of this poison. We have no vaccine. We have no cure.

The Bible teaches that our only hope of avoiding this doom is through Jesus, who died on the cross as a payment for our sin. He took the punishment for sin instead of us, and now we are free to enjoy life with God both now and forever.

As wonderful as this may sound to Christians, atheists and skeptics stand perplexed—offended, even—at the idea that God would send his own Son to be killed and call it good. They may think the story of grace in the Bible sounds barbaric, like an old pagan ritual of blood and sacrifice that should have been buried long ago under the wake of modern sensibilities. Their concerns are many and they deserve our attention. Here are some of their most troublesome questions:

- Isn't it demeaning to call all humanity sinful?
- Are we really saying that God had to abuse his own Son in order to forgive us?
- Why did God even require death in the first place? Couldn't he just forgive?
- How could the death of Jesus be just? Isn't it wrong to have an innocent person bear the penalty a guilty person deserves?

These questions are valid, and they deserve to be answered. The writers of the Bible were careful to articulate why the cross was necessary and what God accomplished on it; they hoped to remove as much misunderstanding as possible. Our goal for this chapter is to follow in their footsteps. With that in mind, we will address the four questions raised above.

Isn't It Demeaning to Call All Humanity Sinful?

The opening illustration to this chapter demonstrated what we identified as a universal truth: Every person on the planet is born with an embedded impulse in his or her heart—a proclivity toward sin.

I (Matthew) once heard a friend say that he could never respect Christians fully because they maintained this dismal outlook on human nature. In his mind, this concept of universal sinfulness was a grievous insult to himself and to the rest of humanity. Many today share his thinking. We often hear it expressed like this: "Sure, I do a few little things I shouldn't now and then, but on the whole, I'm a pretty good person." Though they recognize no one is perfect, they believe the human race is essentially good at heart.

We deceive ourselves far too easily.

Jesus gave a very different diagnosis of the human condition. He looked at the most morally disciplined people of his time and called them "whitewashed tombs," having a nice appearance on the outside but filled with death on the inside.[6] Likewise, he taught that "from the heart come evil thoughts, murder, adultery, all sexual immorality, theft, lying, and slander" (Matthew 15:19). In Jesus's time, the heart was referred to not only as the seat of our emotions, but the seat of our will. It was the center of physical, cognitive, and spiritual life.[7] In other words, the most grievous acts of humanity are not exceptions to our nature. They come from the deepest, truest part of ourselves.

It doesn't matter how presentable we make ourselves on the outside, or even how well we train ourselves to follow our own good intentions. Moralism does nothing to remove our sin or defuse it of its power. It afflicts every human on earth.

Yes, Jesus's teaching on sin may sound demeaning. But the bigger question is whether he was right. Jesus's diagnosis of sin was never intended to insult humanity any more than a cancer diagnosis is intended to insult a sick patient. Quite the contrary, he honored the value of human life by identifying the problem and providing a way forward. As he said in John 3:17 (esv), "God did not send his Son into the world to condemn the world, but in order that the world might be saved through him."

If sin is a serious problem in the human heart with a ready solution available through Jesus, wouldn't we want to know about it? Romans 6:23 tells us the wages of sin is death. Death is the trajectory of sin and its ultimate end. We have encountered a lot of death in this book, not the least of which was in our previous discussion about hell. Sin is to blame for all of it. So it should not surprise us to find that we, who are producers and carriers of sin, should be condemned to die. Remember that God created humanity in his image to be perfect reflections of his nature, deputized to care for his perfect earth. When we rebelled against God, we contaminated ourselves with sin, ruined God's original plan for us, and thus essentially forfeited our reason for existence. We deserved to be wiped off the planet. Sin was deeply embedded within us like an inoperable cancer and by our own free choice. The only way to rid creation of sin was to kill the sinner.

The only problem was that God's love for us far exceeded our rejection of him. In fact, God loved us so deeply that he was willing to do whatever it took to save us from the death we brought down on ourselves. His solution was to send his Son, Jesus, to sound the alarm, alert us to our sin problem, and die on the cross as payment for it. Grace, then, is the free gift of salvation that God provided—not because we deserved it, but because of who God is. This is good news from a good God who aptly proved he would give *anything* so that we would no longer need to face the doom of eternal death.

With this overview of the theology explaining the universality of sin, its nature, and why it was necessary for Jesus to address it, we now respond to the remaining three objections often raised against the sacrificial death of Christ. We hope the ultimate result of this study helps to clarify that the gospel—the good news of Jesus Christ—really does live up to its name!

Is the Cross Divine Child Abuse?

To some, the gospel of God looks like this: God the Father has a temper problem and is really mad at us for becoming sinners. So, he took out all that rage on his own Son. With his anger now expended, he can treat us nicely. The whole scenario comes across as an awful case of domestic child abuse.

Although the death of Jesus is often characterized in this way by atheists and skeptics, Christians reject this view for good reasons. First, it puts God the Father and God the Son at odds with each other. Jesus was insistent that he was one with the Father (John 10:30; 14:8-11), making him fully in tune with the Father's will.

Second, Jesus was not forced or coerced into sacrificing himself for us; he did it willingly and voluntarily. As he said, "The Father loves me because I sacrifice my life so I may take it back again. No one can take my life from me. I sacrifice it voluntarily. For I have the authority to lay it down when I want to and also to take it up again. For this is what my Father has commanded" (John 10:17-18).

Third, when someone takes out his anger on another person, usually it's an impulsive and reactionary act that occurs in the heat of the moment. God's plan for salvation, however, was established long before the world even began (1 Peter 1:18-20).

Fourth, this "angry Father" approach does not explain how the glory of Jesus is connected with his obedience to death (Philippians 2:8-11). If we are seeing the cross as divine child abuse, we are not seeing the cross at all.

In rebuttal, skeptics may ask about the famous prayer Jesus offered in the garden of Gethsemane on the eve of his arrest and execution: "My Father! If it is possible, let this cup of suffering be taken away from me. Yet I want your will to be done, not mine" (Matthew 26:39). This prayer does not show that the Father wanted to kill Jesus while Jesus resisted, kicking and screaming. It does show that Jesus had a natural human wish to avoid suffering, but the text is clear that he willfully gave that up for a greater cause—the will of the Father. Jesus genuinely desired to fulfill the Father's will, even with full knowledge of where that would take him. At the same time, he bore his humanity before God, showing us that his obedience to the cross was not simply a divine magic trick, but a real, brutal experience of death. This is what he endured for our sake.

Another problematic approach to the cross is thinking that God had to punish Jesus before he could love us. This is far from correct. God sent Jesus to die on the cross *because* he loved us (John 3:16). The cross *demonstrates* how much God loves us: "God showed his great love for us by sending Christ to die for us while we were still sinners" (Romans 5:8). In fact, the cross is the key to understanding what love really is: "We know what real love is because Jesus gave up his life for us" (1 John 3:16). God's perfect love is displayed on the cross, and we can understand it this way because the Father and the Son were both freely willing to make the supreme sacrifice for us.

Perhaps part of our misunderstanding comes from the language used to describe how the cross brings forgiveness. In this context, forgiveness refers to the act of God removing our sin from us and declaring us pardoned from the death we deserved. It does not mean God had rancor or ill feelings in his heart toward us prior to the death of Jesus—feelings that somehow went away after Jesus died. Why would God allow his beloved Son to suffer on the cross if his love for us did not exist until after our sins were absolved? Obviously, he loved us dearly and wanted to forgive us even before the cross. Otherwise, he would have had no reason to go through the agony he endured for us.

No, the death of Jesus did not make it possible for God to love us. But it did make it possible for us to see God's love, to know God's love, and to reciprocate that love.

Why Couldn't God Just Forgive Us Without the Cross?

Why did God think it necessary to become a man and endure betrayal, torture, and death in one of the most shameful and horrific ways possible? If God really wanted to save us from the death we brought on ourselves, couldn't he have just waved his hand and declared us forgiven?

It may seem obvious that God, being God, could simply forgive us without dealing with our sin. But this assumption presents its own problems. First, it would contradict God's righteous nature, which we explained in chapter 2. Yes, God is perfectly loving and desires that all people be completely free of their sin. But we must not forget that God is also perfectly holy and perfectly just. As a righteous judge, God will "by no means clear the guilty" (Exodus 34:7 ESV). God punishes sin because he is a God of justice. He isn't soft on serious things, and sin is serious. It is an affront to the holiness of God. It has all the markings of what we call crime in our world—a crime that seriously contaminated the perfection of God's universe. A perfect and holy God cannot allow sin to remain in his perfect creation.

Imagine a judge in our court system who, as an act of love, annulled the charges against every criminal who came before him. As it turns out, we do have such judges in our court system. In mid-September 2021, an activist judge in New York went against the urging of prosecutors and, without even requiring bail, released a man charged with sexual assault. Less than a month later, the released man murdered a nurse. At least three times prior, this same judge had released indicted defendants without requiring bail, and in every case, the released offenders went out and committed additional felonies.[8]

Few of us would want this judge to preside over our own city court. Few would think her lenient policy was either loving or moral. We would rightly be concerned that she failed to take severe crimes seriously. Rather than thinking of her as compassionate to offenders, we would think her callous to the victims and to the safety of society. Did the people of New York praise this judge for her leniency? No, they called for her dismissal and for stricter laws to prevent such leniency as she practiced.

Deep in our hearts, we all want justice. Murder, theft, rape, embezzlement, sex trafficking, and other heinous acts cannot simply be excused. To do that would not be an act of love. Sin is the nexus of pain, suffering, and every act of evil in this world. Sin embeds itself like a cancer in the human heart, which means if God wants to save us, that sin must be removed to stop its continuing contamination and destruction. Knowing this should help us to understand why God demands sin to be dealt with properly and not swept under the rug.

How do we deal properly with sin? As we noted above, "The wages of sin is death" (Romans 6:23). Death is the only fitting punishment for sin committed against a holy God. Death to the sinner ends his growing contamination of God's perfect creation. But God loved us so much that he chose to take the death penalty upon himself rather than enforce it upon humanity. Yes, we still sin, and yes we still experience physical death even after accepting the substitutionary sacrifice of Christ for our sins. But our sins are paid for, and our physical death will be overturned when we are raised to eternal life with sinless perfection in the presence of God. This is good news from a good God who aptly proved he would do whatever it took to forgive us so we would no longer need to face the doom of death we had inflicted upon ourselves.

Despite the necessity of Christ's death to pay for humanity's sin, many question the justice of such an arrangement. This is what we will address in this last section of the chapter.

Isn't Substitutionary Punishment Immoral?

It is easy to understand why someone could see the sacrifice of Christ on the cross as grossly immoral. On the surface, the logic seems turned on its head. If person A commits a crime, how does it serve justice for person B to bear the penalty for it? Even if person B volunteers, justice seems inverted; the innocent is punished and the guilty goes free. The challenge to Christianity is that Jesus is clearly identified as person B in this scenario. We deserved death; he took it in our place. Many have argued this model for justice (called *penal substitution* because Jesus took the penalty as our substitute) only serves to perpetuate wrongdoing rather than correct it. We can understand how difficult it must be to appreciate God's gift of salvation if one cannot shake the feeling that it undermines proper justice.

Christian philosopher William Lane Craig included an important discussion on penal substitution in his book *Atonement and the Death of Christ*. In chapter 10, Craig points out that broadly speaking, there are two theories of justice—retributive and consequentialist. Retributive theories of justice hold that guilty people should be punished simply because they deserve to be punished. Consequentialist theories hold that guilty people should be punished because of the good it produces, such as deterring others from committing the same crime, locking up dangerous people from the rest of society, or providing an opportunity for rehabilitation.

Those who hold to a consequentialist theory should have no problem with the cross because it resulted in a greater good—namely, the offering of God's salvation to the whole world. But Craig points out that this theory is difficult to defend biblically, and we agree. Romans 1:32 and Hebrews 10:29 say the wicked *deserve* punishment, affirming the validity of retributive justice.[9] The consequentialist theory misunderstands justice by imposing on the offender punishment for reasons other than his guilt.

It appears our retributive theories align with God's declaration that guilty humans ought to be punished (Romans 1:32; Hebrews 10:29), and innocent humans ought not to be punished (Genesis 18:25; Deuteronomy 24:16). But can we be sure these theories apply to divine beings in the same way they apply to humans? We are merely human, with human thoughts, emotions, and intuitions. It should be clear that the divine mind of God is far beyond our reach. Given that obvious fact, we should remain open to the idea that, as Craig suggested, God "reserves the prerogative to punish an innocent *divine* person, namely, Christ, in the place of the guilty"[10] (emphasis ours).

We can see a possible logic in God allowing a sinless divine being to take the punishment for guilty humanity. It works like this: Divine love wants to save humanity, and the only way it can be done and yet satisfy divine justice is for a being with no guilt to take upon himself the guilt of humanity. God has no guilt, and so God volunteers to become a man so he can take humanity's guilt as his own and die for it, thus allowing humanity to go free. The Bible tells us clearly that Jesus did indeed take upon himself the guilt of humanity (2 Corinthians 5:21; 1 Peter 2:24). This is what Christians mean when they say our sins were "imputed" to Christ at the cross. All the guilt of our sin extended onto him.

This imputation of sin to the innocent was not immoral because Jesus willingly volunteered to take the load.

Now, here is the key that keeps this substitutionary transaction from being an immoral miscarriage of justice: *By virtue of the imputation, all of Jesus's inherited sin would make him exceedingly guilty before God. Because Jesus was made guilty, his punishment was justified.* When his punishment was complete, all the guilt he bore—our guilt—was fully paid for, making us exceedingly innocent before God. Because we were made innocent, our lack of punishment is justified. Seen from this perspective, it is clear that God saving humanity by means of penal substitution does not demonstrate a lack of his moral integrity. To the contrary, it is an amazing demonstration of sheer love.

We may look at imputation and struggle to understand how a morally innocent person could take on the guilt of sin, thereby allowing him to pay the penalty for those who actually committed the sin. However, the extension of guilt to include an additional person is not totally foreign to our way of thinking. Consider the concept of *vicarious liability.* This term is applied in legal situations where someone who is responsible for the offender is made responsible for the offense. For example, employers are often held responsible for offenses committed by their employees.[11] A customer who is shopping in a department store and is injured by a janitor dropping a bucket from a ladder will sue the store owner, not the janitor. In like manner, we could say that God, who created humanity, willed for himself to take on responsibility for humanity. He cosigned our loans and paid the debt that we lacked the resources to repay. As our creator, he is uniquely positioned to do this.

One other explanation for the sacrifice of Christ is called the ransom theory. Christ said he came "to give his life as a ransom for many" (Matthew 20:28), and Paul affirms that he accomplished that feat (1 Timothy 2:6). According to this theory, when Adam and Eve sinned in Eden, they forfeited their lives to the tempter, Satan, who has a vendetta against God and hates humanity as God's favored creation. Satan intended to destroy humanity, but Christ offered himself as a ransom, saying, in effect, "Take me instead." Satan jumped at the chance, possibly thinking that by killing Christ he would destroy the godhead and become ruler of heaven and earth. But he didn't anticipate the resurrection, which saved mankind and ultimately rendered Satan powerless.

Several other reasons could be given to justify the sacrifice of Jesus on our behalf.[12] The Bible itself does not explain or endorse any one theory. But we don't need to understand fully *how* Jesus's sacrifice works; we simply need to recognize that it *works*. By analogy, most of us have no idea how the chips, circuits, cards, and switches inside our computers provide the images we see on our screens. Yet our computers work for us despite our lack of understanding.

If you can simply trust that Christ died for your sins, that is all the knowledge you really need. Let's stop sitting in our unlocked cells complaining that God should have saved us by some other method that does not offend our sensibilities. Instead, let's marvel at the goodness of God, who acted self-sacrificially for our sake.

The Perfect Blend of Justice and Love

Several years ago, I (Matthew) was invited to teach on apologetics and evangelism at a church in northern Minnesota.

During my stay there, an old friend from college learned I was in town and generously invited me to breakfast. As an atheist, he expressed difficulty with the cross because it seemed to remove from us any need for moral responsibility. If Christ's sacrifice removed the guilt for all our misdeeds, why would we bother to behave morally?

I remember looking across the table at his daughter, whom I will call Emma. At the time, Emma was about one year old. I asked my friend to imagine that he had a $5,000 television set, and after Emma grew to be three or four years old, she somehow managed to knock the TV over and break it. I asked my friend what he would do in this situation. Emma might realize that she had done something bad and want to fix the problem by forfeiting her dollar-a-week allowance. But a child that age would have no ability to comprehend the size of her debt, let alone pay it! As a father, my friend might wish to teach Emma responsibility by ordering her to pay for the broken television, but he would realize this was impossible. He would have to pay for the damages himself. All the while, he would hope that Emma would know she is forgiven and Daddy still loves her.

Despite all the bad things you have done, God loves you. Pause and consider this for a moment: For some, the three words *God loves you* have been repeated so much they have lost their meaning. For others, the words are so foreign that they find no meaning in them at all. But nothing in all this world could be richer, more astonishing, more outrageous, than the idea that the God of this universe has chosen to love us, even to the point of coming to earth and paying a debt too great for us to comprehend.

God's love and justice blend together in full display on the cross of Jesus. Here, we see him uncompromising in his justice.

Sin *has* to be dealt with. At the same time, God's love and mercy shine through in all their blinding light. Here, we see Jesus willingly stretch out his arms and endure one of the most horrific modes of death ever devised by the human race. Writhing in pain and gazing upon his jeering crowd of hecklers and tormentors, Jesus, through his gasps of agony, managed to utter a simple but astounding prayer. You will never understand the goodness of God until you understand the depth of his words: "Father, forgive them, for they don't know what they are doing" (Luke 23:34).

Even after hearing these words of love, the crowd continued to mock him. They had no idea that they were witnessing the most profound moment in all human history.

We should remember that Jesus was not the only one nailed to a cross that morning. Two others, both criminals, were executed beside him. According to Luke, one of the criminals fell in with the crowd and mocked Jesus. However, "the other criminal protested, 'Don't you fear God even when you have been sentenced to die? We deserve to die for our crimes, but this man hasn't done anything wrong.' Then he said, 'Jesus, remember me when you come into your Kingdom.' And Jesus replied, 'I assure you, today you will be with me in paradise'" (Luke 23:40-43).

While many continue to mock God because he allowed an innocent man to die for the guilt of others, this unnamed criminal accepted Jesus *because* of his innocence. And just like that, he was immediately wiped clean—no longer contaminated from a lifetime of sin and now established as a son in the family of God. Unfortunately, he did not have much life left to live on earth. We can only imagine what sort of amazing adventures he would have had telling others about his freedom from guilt, made possible by the sacrifice of a just and loving God. Nevertheless, that one moment with Christ marked the beginning of his life. It all began when he refused to follow the voices of those around him, acknowledged the guilt of his sin, and threw himself on the mercy of a good God.

Epilogue:

Good News from a Good God

What comes into our minds when we think about God
is the most important thing about us.[1]

—A.W. TOZER

The book of Revelation is frightening. In this last book in the
Bible, God's judgments and the second coming of Jesus are
described. The sun and sky are darkened (Revelation 9:2). Hail
and fire mixed with blood hurtle down to earth (Revelation 8:7).
Swarms of locusts with scorpion-like stingers rise up from a smoking abyss to torment people for five months (Revelation 9:3-5). This
was only the beginning of God's judgment over sinful humanity!

Many theologians consider these events to be metaphoric
because the apocalyptic genre of Revelation is highly symbolic.
Even from that perspective, they are no less difficult to swallow. The stories of judgment in Revelation include some of the
most vivid descriptions of human agony in the Bible. Any view
that God's severity is merely an Old Testament phenomenon is
immediately put to rest.

And yet, as we learned throughout this book, a good God
has good reasons for judgment. He is holy, and his desire is for

everyone to be saved from his wrath. The fact is, we could go on about different challenges we encounter in the Bible, but there comes a point when we have enough understanding to believe that God is truly good, even in light of the passages of Scripture that seem to convey otherwise. So, what now?

Perhaps it is time to start reading these stories of judgment as they were originally intended to be heard—as a signal to recognize the severity of our sin, to fall on our knees, and surrender ourselves to the mercy of a good and holy God.

Contrary to popular religion, we cannot be saved by good works any more than we can reach the moon by jumping off a chair. We all have turned away from God, sinning against him through disobedience, and no amount of good behavior will change that fact. But God loves us so much that he sent his Son, Jesus, who died on the cross for our sins and rose again. We can receive this free gift of forgiveness through faith in Jesus—that is, believing and trusting in his power to save us, rather than striving in our own power. As the Bible proudly declares, "It is by grace you have been saved, through faith—and this is not from yourselves, it is the gift of God—not by works, so that no one can boast" (Ephesians 2:8-9 NIV).

Those who believe and trust in Jesus are not just saved *from* their sins; they are saved *to* God. When we say yes to God, we are saying yes to new life with him. He becomes king and we submit to his "good, pleasing and perfect will" (Romans 12:2 NIV). Likewise, we are saved *to* God's family, the church, where God forms us together to become more obedient to him. As we pursue this new life with God, we can trust that he is present, graciously guiding us along every step of the way.

If you have never decided to trust in Jesus, we invite you to make that decision right now, wherever you are reading this book. If you are ready and you would like some guidance in expressing yourself to God, then you can pray these words:

Lord Jesus, I want to begin a relationship with you. I'm sorry for my sins. Thank you for dying on the cross to remove them. I don't deserve your sacrifice, but I'm grateful that you willingly died for me. I receive your gift of forgiveness and commit to following you daily as my King and Savior. Thank you so much for seeing me as worthy and loveable. I now understand that you are really, truly good. Amen.

If you have already decided to trust in Jesus or you have done so just now, consider the journey we have taken. In chapter 1, we introduced you to Isaac Asimov, who boldly stated, "Properly read, [the Bible] is the most potent force for atheism ever conceived." His sentiment toward the Bible is common, and even many Christians have worried that he might be right. But in chapter 2, we began addressing the difficult passages of the Bible by starting at the beginning, in the book of Genesis. We saw the tragedy of when Adam and Eve sinned and lost the presence of God. Over the course of this book, we witnessed the continued effect of sin as we worked through the Old Testament and eventually into the New Testament. Now, in the book of Revelation, we are confronted again with God's severity against sin. But at the same time, we see that the Christian's story ends in triumph. Jesus returns! He renders judgment against evil, he destroys the powers of death and darkness, and then it happens:

Then I saw "a new heaven and a new earth," for the first heaven and the first earth had passed away, and there was no longer any sea. I saw the Holy City, the new Jerusalem, coming down out of heaven from God, prepared as a bride beautifully dressed for her husband. And I heard a loud voice from the throne saying, "Look! God's dwelling place is now among the people, and he will dwell with them. They will be his people, and God himself will be with them and be their God" (Revelation 21:1-3).

And so, looking forward to this day, we can be confident with a rock-solid conviction that God truly is good. He is always good. There is nothing in the Bible for which we need to apologize. There is no reason for us to be ashamed. In fact, we can help others to understand this too. We can show them something they may have never expected to see: That properly read, the Bible is the most potent force for the good news of Jesus ever conceived.

Notes

Chapter 1—Just How Good Is God?

1. Cited in Janet J. Asimov, *Notes for a Memoir: On Isaac Asimov, Life, and Writing* (Amherst, NY: Prometheus Books, 2006), 58.

2. Micah Lang, "Should I Raise My Hands in Worship?," *Relevant*, January 15, 2014, https://relevantmagazine.com/god/church/should-i-raise-my-hands-worship. Accessed July 16, 2020.

3. Adapted from Amy Watkins, "Having a baby made me an atheist," offbeathome.com, https://offbeathome.com/atheist-parent/. Accessed June 28, 2021.

4. Adapted from Jeremy Myers, "Bible Verses that Turn Christians into Atheists," patheos.com, April 27, 2016, https://www.patheos.com/blogs/unfundamentalistchristians/2016/04/11-bible-verses-that-turn-christians-into-atheists/. Accessed June 28, 2021.

5. David Plotz, "Good Book: What I learned from reading the entire Bible," slate.com, http://www.slate.com/articles/news_and_politics/blogging_the_bible/2009/03/good_book.html. Accessed June 28, 2021.

6. Richard Dawkins, *The God Delusion* (Boston, MA: Houghton Mifflin, 2008), 51.

7. See Dawkins, *The God Delusion*, 283-284.

8. Explicit statements asserting God's goodness are found in 1 Chronicles 16:34; 2 Chronicles 5:13; 6:41; 7:3; 30:18; Ezra 3:11; Psalms 25:8; 34:8; 86:5; 100:5; 106:1; 107:1; 118:1, 29; 119:68; 135:3; 136:1; Jeremiah 33:11; Nahum 1:7; Mark 10:18; Luke 18:19. Depending how one chooses to translate, the same idea is implicitly stated in Matthew 19:17, Romans 2:4, and 1 Peter 2:3. This list does not include all the passages that mention the attributes of God that we already consider to be good, such as his righteousness, faithfulness, lovingkindness, patience, graciousness, mercifulness, and generosity.

9. Fyodor Dostoevsky, *The Brothers Karamazov* (New York: Farrar, Straus and Giroux, 1990), 489.

10. Joshua Ryan Butler, *The Skeletons in God's Closet: The Mercy of Hell, the Surprise of Judgment, the Hope of Holy War* (Nashville, TN: Thomas Nelson, 2014).

11. Cited in Janet J. Asimov, *Notes for a Memoir: on Isaac Asimov, Life, and Writing* (Amherst, NY: Prometheus Books, 2006), 58.

12. This happens in Exodus 22 after the people of Israel worship a golden calf.

13. Christopher Hitchens, *God Is Not Great: How Religion Poisons Everything* (New York: Twelve, 2009), 99. Hitchens was commenting on the Sabbath command in Exodus 20:8-11.

Chapter 2—Humanity's Rough Beginnings

1. Mikhail Bakunin, *God and the State,* 1871, https://www.marxists.org/reference/archive/bakunin/works/godstate/ch02.htm. Accessed 3/2/2021.

2. John C. Lennox, *Gunning for God: Why the New Atheists Are Missing the Target* (Oxford: Lion, 2011), 134.

3. Quoted in: Glenn Miller, "God apparently set humanity up for failure in the Garden, so doesn't this show Him to be cruel, schizoid, or psychotic?," *A Christian ThinkTank,* November 2, 1998, http://www.christian-thinktank.com/gutripper.html. Accessed May 10, 2021.

4. Genesis 6:4 mentions the Nephilim or Nephilites dwelling on the earth. The ancient Greek translation of the text called them "giants," whereas a literal meaning of the Hebrew is "fallen ones."

5. This is apparent because of Genesis 6:3, where God limits the time of humanity in response to the sons of God taking wives. We also see this material being used contextually as background leading up to God's decision to destroy humanity.

6. This idea comes from Genesis 3:15, the so-called protoevangelium. Though it uses cryptic language, the meaning was clarified and the promise fulfilled when Christ triumphed over Satan through his death and resurrection on the cross.

7. Second Peter 2:5 calls Noah a "herald of righteousness" (esv), which the NLT smooths out by saying "Noah warned the world of God's righteous judgment."

8. For example, Lot offered his two daughters to be raped to appease the mob in Sodom (Genesis 19:8), but the angelic visitors would not

compromise that way (verses 10-11). The family was hesitant to follow the angels' instructions (verse 16), Lot's wife disobeyed by looking back to see the destruction (verse 26), and his daughters got him drunk, seduced him, and impregnated themselves with him (verses 30-38).

9. See Exodus 1:22–2:3.

10. Cf. Genesis 2:17 with Genesis 3:23.

11. This was forewarned incessantly over many years by the prophets' spoken and written messages, such as the one recorded in Jeremiah 13:15-27.

12. The entire story of Jonah is about God calling a prophet to warn the city of Nineveh of judgment. The Ninevites repented, and God relented from executing judgment.

13. Jesus spoke frequently of judgment. See Matthew 24–25, or Luke 10:10-16. Paul also spoke of God's judgment in Romans 1:18-32 and elsewhere.

Chapter 3—When "Holy War" Doesn't Sound Holy

1. Dan Barker, *God: The Most Unpleasant Character in All Fiction* (New York: Sterling, 2016), timecode 28:35–29:10 in Audible.

2. Paul Copan, *Is God a Moral Monster? Making Sense of the Old Testament God* (Grand Rapids, MI: Baker Books, 2011), 23.

3. See Joshua 13–21.

4. Charlie Trimm, "YHWH & Genocide," Talbot Magazine—Biola University Blogs, June 15, 2017, https://www.biola.edu/blogs/talbot-magazine/2017/yhwh-and-genocide.

5. E.g., Ezra 3:11; Psalms 100:5; 119:68; Nahum 1:7; Mark 10:18.

6. See Malachi 3:6; James 1:17.

7. C.S. Lewis, *The Lion, the Witch and the Wardrobe* (New York: Macmillan, 1950), 64.

8. See Deuteronomy 9:4; cf. Ezra 8:22; Psalms 18:25-26.

9. Examples would include Thom Stark, *The Human Faces of God: What Scripture Reveals When It Gets God Wrong* (Eugene, OR: Wipf and Stock, 2011). Eric A. Seibert, *Disturbing Divine Behavior: Troubling Old Testament Images of God* (Minneapolis, MN: Fortress Press, 2011). Derek Flood, *Disarming Scripture: Cherry-Picking Liberals, Violence-Loving Conservatives, and Why We All Need to Learn to Read the Bible Like Jesus Did* (San Francisco, CA: Metanoia Press, 2014). Peter Enns, *The Bible Tells Me So: Why Defending Scripture Has Made Us Unable to Read It* (New York: HarperOne, 2015).

10. 1 Peter 1:10-12.

11. Matthew 11:27; John 1:17-18.

12. Peter C. Craigie, *The Book of Deuteronomy*, The New International Commentary on the Old Testament (Grand Rapids, MI: Wm. B. Eerdmans, 1976), 177.

13. David T. Lamb, *God Behaving Badly: Is the God of the Old Testament Angry, Sexist, and Racist?* (Downers Grove, IL: IVP Books, 2011), 100.

14. See John H. Walton and J. Harvey Walton, *The Lost World of the Israelite Conquest: Covenant, Retribution, and the Fate of the Canaanites* (Downers Grove, IL: IVP Academic, 2017), part 5.

15. Jeremiah considered this to be a general truism of war when he wrote, "At the noise of charioteers and archers, the people flee in terror. They hide in the bushes and run for the mountains. All the towns have been abandoned—not a person remains!" (Jeremiah 4:29).

16. Jericho is called a city in Joshua 6:3. Ai is called a city in Joshua 8:1.

17. Ludwig Koehler et al., *The Hebrew and Aramaic Lexicon of the Old Testament* (Leiden: E.J. Brill, 1994–2000), s.v. "רִיק".

18. See Joshua 6:15-17.

19. See Richard Hess, "The Jericho and Ai in the Book of Joshua," in *Critical Issues in Early Israelite History* (Winona Lake, IN: Eisenbrauns, 2008) and also "War in the Hebrew Bible: An Overview" in *War in the Bible and Terrorism in the Twenty-First Century* (Winona Lake, IN: Eisenbrauns, 2008). We should add that Richard Hess is a conservative Old Testament scholar at Denver Seminary, and he is no lightweight in these matters. His commentary on the book of Joshua is scored the highest ranking on bestcommentaries.com.

20. See Hess, Klingbeil, and Ray, eds., *Critical Issues in Early Israelite History*, 46.

21. Hess, Klingbeil, and Ray, eds., *Critical Issues in Early Israelite History*, 41-42, 46. See also the note for Joshua 8:3 in the *IVP Bible Background Commentary*, eds. John H. Walton, Victor H. Matthews, and Mark W. Chavalas (Downers Grove, IL: IVP Academic, 2000).

22. This was commonly understood in its time. Paul Copan gives a list of other cultures which employed the same kind of exaggerated rhetoric in *Is God a Moral Monster?* (Grand Rapids, MI: Baker, 2011), 172.

23. Some loose translations try to smoothen this out, but the strong contrast is present in the original Hebrew.

24. For examples, see Paul Copan, *Is God a Moral Monster?*, 170ff; John Lennox, *Gunning for God*, 129; Kevin Lawson Younger Jr., "The Rhetorical Structuring of the Joshua Conquest Narratives," in *Critical Issues in Early Israelite History*, 15; Joshua Butler, *The Skeletons in God's Closet* (Nashville, TN: Thomas Nelson, 2014), 228ff.

25. According to historian Shelby Brown, "The Carthaginian practice was indeed unique, combining infanticide and human sacrifice in a way unacceptable to others" (Susanna Shelby Brown, *Late Carthaginian Child Sacrifice and Sacrificial Monuments in Their Mediterranean Context*, JSOT/ASOR Monograph Series, no. 3 [Sheffield, England: Published by JSOT Press for the American Schools of Oriental Research, 1991], 175.) Carthaginians were Phoenicians who, according to W.F. Albright, are synonymous with the Canaanites (see Albright, *The Bible and the Ancient Near East: Essays in Honor of William Foxwell Albright* [Winona Lake, IN: Eisenbrauns, 1979], 438.)

26. This is talked about in Leviticus 18. See also Clay Jones, "We Don't Hate Sin So We Don't Understand What Happened to the Canaanites" (*Philosophia Christi*, Vol. 11, 2009).

27. See Deuteronomy 7:4; 20:16-18.

28. See Judges 2:11-13; Jeremiah 19:4-5. See also G.F. Moore in *The Journal of Biblical Lit. XVI* (1897), https://penelope.uchicago.edu/Thayer/E/Journals/JBL/16/Biblical_Notes/Image_of_Moloch*.html.

29. Deuteronomy 12:31 shows that the Israelites understood this to be the case.

30. Plutarch, *On Superstition*, https://penelope.uchicago.edu/Thayer/E/Roman/Texts/Plutarch/Moralia/De_superstitione*.html. For evidence connecting this to Canaanite society, see G.F. Moore in *The Journal of Biblical Lit. XVI* (1897), https://penelope.uchicago.edu/Thayer/E/Journals/JBL/16/Biblical_Notes/Image_of_Moloch*.html.

31. According to Clay Jones, "Brown cites archaeological evidence that many thousands of children were victims" (Clay Jones, "We Don't Hate Sin So We Don't Understand What Happened to the Canaanites" (*Philosophia Christi*, Vol. 11, 2009, footnote 38).

32. See Deuteronomy 7:1.

33. Numbers 13–14 describe the Israelites' fear when they first checked out the land of Canaan. Their cowardice showed up again in Joshua 7:5.

34. The battle against Jericho in Joshua 6 is a prime example of their nonsensical strategies. It goes to show that God was fighting for them.

35. See George E. Mendenhall, "Amorites," ed. David Noel Freedman, *The Anchor Yale Bible Dictionary* (New York: Doubleday, 1992), 199.

36. In Genesis 15, God told Abraham there would be 400 years of waiting, "for the sins of the Amorites do not yet warrant their destruction" (Genesis 15:16b). "Amorites" is another word for the inhabitants of Canaan.

37. See Ezekiel 33:11 and Lamentations 3:32-33.

38. Rahab is given 720 words in the Hebrew text of Joshua 2 and Joshua 6:22-25. The rest of Joshua 6 is the battle of Jericho, consisting of 589 words. These word counts were conducted on the text of BHS with the Concordance tool of Logos Bible Software. (Note that not all words in Hebrew are separated by a space.)

39. See John Nolland's commentary of Matthew 1:5 in the *New International Greek Testament Commentary* (Grand Rapids, MI: Eerdmans, 2005).

40. See Hebrews 11:31 and James 2:25.

Chapter 4—The Bible's Immoral Heroes

1. Richard Dawkins, *The God Delusion* (Boston, MA: Houghton Mifflin, 2008), 268.

2. J. Kent Edwards, *Effective First-Person Biblical Preaching: The Steps from Text to Narrative Sermon* (Grand Rapids, MI: Zondervan, 2005), 31.

3. The number of wives David married might actually exceed this number, but at least eight of them are explicitly mentioned (1 Samuel 18:27; 25:42-43; 2 Samuel 3:3-5; 11:27; 1 Chronicles 3:1-9).

4. James A. Brooks, *Mark*, vol. 23, The New American Commentary (Nashville: Broadman & Holman Publishers, 1991), 62.

5. See Mark 2:15. NLT reads "scum," but the original Greek reads tax collectors and sinners.

6. Deuteronomy 7:3 commands against intermarriage. The reason is provided in the following verse. It is not because of racism, but because the religion of their neighbors would lead them away from God.

7. See Judges 13:1.

8. Preston Sprinkle, *Charis: God's Scandalous Grace for Us*, Kindle Edition (Colorado Springs, CO: David C. Cook, 2014), 28.

9. A person who made a rash vow could confess the sin and bring a sin offering, not following through with the action. See Leviticus 5:4-6.

10. It is an abomination in God's eyes to sacrifice children. See Leviticus 18:21; Deuteronomy 18:10.

11. See Genesis 29:31–30:24. These children became the fathers of the 12 tribes of Israel.

12. See 1 Kings 11:1-8.

13. According to the *Faithlife Study Bible*, "David inherited Saul's harem, symbolizing that he had seized the throne (compare 2 Sam 3:7 and note; 16:22)." John D. Barry, Douglas Mangum, et al., *Faithlife Study Bible* (Bellingham, WA: Lexham Press, 2012, 2016), 2 Samuel 12:8.

14. According to commentator Joyce Baldwin, "Evidently the custom was that the harem of the dead monarch was inherited by his successor, and by this rule David had already added to his household." Joyce G. Baldwin, *1 and 2 Samuel: An Introduction and Commentary*, vol. 8, Tyndale Old Testament Commentaries (Downers Grove, IL: Inter-Varsity Press, 1988), 254.

15. Carl E. DeVries, "Imprecatory Psalms," *Baker Encyclopedia of the Bible* (Grand Rapids, MI: Baker, 1988), 1023.

Chapter 5—The Traumatic Tests of Abraham and Job

1. Thomas Nagel, *The Last Word* (Oxford: Oxford University Press, 2001), 130.

2. Michael L. Brown, *Hyper-Grace* (Lake Mary, FL: Charisma House, 2014), 127.

3. Rachel Held Evans, "I Would Fail Abraham's Test (and I Bet You Would Too)," October 14, 2014, https://rachelheldevans.com/blog/fail-abraham-test. Accessed July 14, 2020.

4. Victor P. Hamilton, *The Book of Genesis, Chapters 18–50*, The New International Commentary on the Old Testament (Grand Rapids, MI: Wm. B. Eerdmans, 1995), 101.

5. See Hebrews 11:17-19.

6. Faith is a gift from God, according to Ephesians 2:8. See also Romans 10:17 and Hebrews 12:2.

7. See Genesis 22:2, 6.

8. Abraham was 100 years old when Isaac was born, according to Genesis 21:5.

9. See Ellen F. Davis, "Self-Consciousness and Conversation: Reading Genesis 22," ed. Bruce Chilton, *Bulletin for Biblical Research*, Vol. 1 (1991): 36. She cites the Genesis Rabbah 56.8 as the Jewish Midrash that delivers this interpretation.

10. Luther's Works, Volume 4, *Lectures on Genesis,* 119-120, as cited in Barbara Owen, *Steadfast in Your Word* (Minneapolis, MN: Augsburg Fortress, 2002), 5.

11. See John 1:29; also 1 Corinthians 5:7.

12. John 19:17 notes that Jesus carried his own cross, though some of the synoptics add that Simon of Cyrene also helped.

13. The Bible does not say that Jesus went up a mountain to be crucified. But it identifies his location as Golgotha, which, in Latin, is where we get "Calvary mountain." Tradition has understood this place to be a mountain. Regardless, there are many stories in the life of Christ where he does go up a mountain, especially during a theological climax.

14. This is the number that I (Matthew) came up with after counting from the ESV.

15. Ellen F. Davis, *Getting Involved with God: Rediscovering the Old Testament* (Cambridge, MA: Cowley Publications, 2001), 124.

16. I heard him say this during a class lecture on the book of Job.

17. Job 28, famously dubbed the "Ode to Wisdom," is at the center, situated between the two long discourse sections, which, in turn, are positioned between the opening and closing narratives. The technical term for this kind of literary structure, where a series of components is repeated in reverse order, is a chiasm. It was quite common in Bible times, and its placement at the center of the structure was often intended for greater emphasis.

18. Ellen Davis, observing that dust and ashes are always presented as a metaphor in Scripture, suggests a better translation of Job 42:6 to be "Therefore I recant and change my mind concerning dust and ashes." See Davis, *Getting Involved with God,* 141.

19. Davis, *Getting Involved with God,* 141.

20. Fred L. Horton Jr., "Inheritance," Holman Illustrated Bible Dictionary, eds. Chad Brand, Charles Draper, Archie England, Steve Bond, E. Ray Clendenen, and Trent C. Butler (Nashville, TN: Holman Bible Publishers, 2003).

Chapter 6—Wise Legislator or Oppressive Dictator?

1. Sam Harris, *The End of Faith: Religion, Terror, and the Future of Reason* (New York: W.W. Norton & Co., 2005), 82.

2. David T. Lamb, *God Behaving Badly: Is the God of the Old Testament Angry, Sexist, and Racist?* (Downers Grove, IL: IVP Books, 2011), 121.

3. Ronald L. Eisenberg, *The JPS Guide to Jewish Traditions* (Philadelphia, PA: The Jewish Publication Society, 2004), 515-516.

4. Impact 360 Institute, *Gen Z Vol. 2* (Barna report produced in partnership with Impact 360 Institute) (Pine Mountain, GA: Impact 360 Institute, 2021), 52.

5. See Muhammad A. Dandamayev, "Slavery: Old Testament," ed. David Noel Freedman, *The Anchor Yale Bible Dictionary* (New York: Doubleday, 1992), 63.

6. Ludwig Koehler et al., *The Hebrew and Aramaic Lexicon of the Old Testament* (Leiden: E.J. Brill, 1994–2000), s.v. "דְּבַק".

7. Helmer Ringgren, U. Rüterswörden, and H. Simian-Yofre, "דָּבַק," eds. G. Johannes Botterweck and Heinz-Josef Fabry, trans. Douglas W. Stott, *Theological Dictionary of the Old Testament* (Grand Rapids, MI; Cambridge, U.K.: William B. Eerdmans Publishing Company, 1999), 387.

8. Muhammad A. Dandamayev, "Slavery: Old Testament," ed. David Noel Freedman, *The Anchor Yale Bible Dictionary* (New York: Doubleday, 1992), 65.

9. According to Richard Melick, "Many slaves took every opportunity to run from their masters. They normally fled to large cities, eating whatever they could and hiding from the authorities who might recognize them. Thus, freedom brought a worse life than they had had with their masters. In addition, the penalty for runaway slaves was severe." See: Richard R. Melick, *Philippians, Colossians, Philemon*, vol. 32, The New American Commentary (Nashville, TN: Broadman & Holman Publishers, 1991), 343.

10. Some do not think that Onesimus was a runaway slave. But there are strong reasons to believe otherwise. For example, see: Nordling, John G. 1991. "Onesimus Fugitivus: A Defense of the Runaway Slave Hypothesis in Philemon," *Journal for the Study of the New Testament* 13 (41): 97-119.

11. "Worship (n.)," Online Etymology Dictionary, https://www.etymonline.com/word/worship. Accessed July 16, 2020.

12. Micah Lang, "Should I Raise My Hands in Worship?," *Relevant Magazine,* January 15, 2014, https://relevantmagazine.com/god/church/should-i-raise-my-hands-worship. Accessed July 16, 2020.

13. This view of human flourishing will be discussed in the next chapter.

14. I (Matthew) came up with this count when I set out to study every verse that addresses the topic of fearing God.

15. Sometimes the best translation in certain situations is "reverence" or "respect," but in most cases, "fear" is the best translation.

16. See Stuart D. Sacks, "Fear," *Baker Encyclopedia of the Bible* (Grand Rapids, MI: Baker, 1988), 781.

17. See Paul Copan, *Is God a Moral Monster?* (Grand Rapids, MI: Baker, 2011), 95, where he cites Walter Kaiser, Raymond Westbook, Jacob Finkelstein, and Joseph Sprinke.

18. John Goldingay, *Old Testament Ethics: A Guided Tour* (Downers Grove, IL: InterVarsity Press, 2019), 4-5.

19. In Genesis 1:27-28, God made humankind distinct by making them in his image and giving them dominion over the animals.

20. See Exodus 23:12.

21. René Péter-Contesse and John Ellington, *A Handbook on Leviticus,* UBS Handbook Series (New York: United Bible Societies, 1992), 91.

22. "Bleeding," Humane Slaughter Association, https://www.hsa.org.uk/bleeding-and-pithing/bleeding. Accessed July 17, 2020.

23. See Leviticus 1–7. The only offering that did not require eating the animal was the burnt offering.

24. Cornelius Plantinga Jr., *Not the Way It's Supposed to Be: A Breviary of Sin* (Grand Rapids, MI: Eerdmans, 1996), 95.

25. For examples, see chapter 8 of *Toward Old Testament Ethics* by Walter Kaiser Jr. (Grand Rapids, MI: Zondervan, 1991), or chapter 8 of *A Survey of the Old Testament,* 3rd ed., by Andrew Hill and John Walton (Grand Rapids, MI: Zondervan, 2009).

26. According to the original Hebrew, the Ten Commandments are actually the Ten "Words" or "Statements." In light of this, some theological traditions divide the ten statements differently, but it's the same text in each case.

27. Sean McDowell, "What Does the Bible Say About Homosexuality? Sean McDowell and Matthew Vines in Conversation," February 3, 2018, video, 2:10:34, https://www.youtube.com/watch?v=yFY4VtCWgyI, 12:38.

Chapter 7—How Law Became Life

1. Christopher Hitchens, *God Is Not Great: How Religion Poisons Everything* (New York: Twelve, 2009), 38.

2. Kevin DeYoung and Ted Kluck, *Why We're Not Emergent: By Two Guys Who Should Be* (Chicago IL: Moody, 2008), 84.

3. R.G. Branch, "Eve," *Dictionary of the Old Testament: Pentateuch,* eds. T. Desmond Alexander and David W. Baker (Downers Grove, IL: InterVarsity Press, 2003), 240.

4. For examples, see Genesis 6:3, Psalm 56:13, Romans 4:17, and 1 Timothy 6:13.

5. Robert Anderson Street, "Eden," *Holman Illustrated Bible Dictionary,* eds. Chad Brand et al., (Nashville, TN: Holman Bible Publishers, 2003), 458.

6. See Genesis 3:22-24.

7. Many commentators suggest this farther move of Cain given the theological nature of Genesis and that the garden's entrance was guarded on the east side (Genesis 3:24).

8. L. Michael Morales, *Who Shall Ascend the Mountain of the Lord?: A Biblical Theology of the Book of Leviticus* (Downers Grove, IL: InterVarsity Press, 2015), 49.

9. Technically, "I will come to you" is only four words in Hebrew.

10. Compare Genesis 2:8; 3:24 with Exodus 27:13; Leviticus 1:16; 16:14.

11. See Gregory K. Beale, "Eden, the Temple, and the Church's Mission in the New Creation," *Journal of the Evangelical Theological Society* 48, no. 1 (2005): 8.

12. For a fuller discussion of the tabernacle and the garden, see L. Michael Morales, *Who Shall Ascend the Mountain of the Lord?: A Biblical Theology of the Book of Leviticus* (Downers Grove, IL: InterVarsity Press, 2015), chapter 2. On the temple, see Gregory K. Beale, "Eden, the Temple, and the Church's Mission in the New Creation," *Journal of the Evangelical Theological Society* 48, no. 1 (2005).

13. Gordon J. Wenham, *Numbers: An Introduction and Commentary,* vol. 4, Tyndale Old Testament Commentaries (Downers Grove, IL: InterVarsity Press, 1981), 107.

14. L. Michael Morales, *Who Shall Ascend the Mountain of the Lord?: A Biblical Theology of the Book of Leviticus* (Downers Grove, IL: InterVarsity Press, 2015), 17.

15. Technically, the first word is the conjunction *waw,* which often functions like the English word *and.*

16. C.S. Lewis, *Mere Christianity,* from The C.S. Lewis Signature Classics (San Francisco, CA: HarperOne, 2017). 43.

17. The following examples are taken from Victor Harold Matthews, Mark W. Chavalas, and John H. Walton, *The IVP Bible Background Commentary: Old Testament,* electronic ed. (Downers Grove, IL:

InterVarsity Press, 2000) and from Gordon J. Wenham, *The Book of Leviticus,* The New International Commentary on the Old Testament (Grand Rapids, MI: Wm. B. Eerdmans, 1979).

18. Technically, leaven is anything that causes bread to rise. For this reason, people often say that leaven was yeast. But in Israel's time, the people actually mixed a bit of old, fermented dough with fresh dough. This is how they caused their bread to rise.

19. L. Michael Morales, *Who Shall Ascend the Mountain of the Lord?: A Biblical Theology of the Book of Leviticus* (Downers Grove, IL: InterVarsity Press, 2015), 145.

20. See Isaiah 1:16; Ezekiel 36:25.

21. Sometimes the remedy for uncleanliness involves a "sin offering," but this would be better translated as a "purification offering." Leviticus distinguishes these kinds of offerings from the offerings that deal with actual sin in chapters 4–7.

22. See Leviticus 20:23-26.

23. For example, diseases often required washing and social distancing for some time. Unclean animals often carried diseases.

24. Paul Copan, *Is God a Moral Monster?: Making Sense of the Old Testament God* (Grand Rapids, MI: Baker, 2011), 81-83.

25. L. Michael Morales, *Who Shall Ascend the Mountain of the Lord?: A Biblical Theology of the Book of Leviticus* (Downers Grove, IL: InterVarsity Press, 2015), 158.

26. Morales, *Who Shall Ascend the Mountain of the Lord?*

27. Probably the majority of scholars view the Day of Atonement to be the literary center of how Leviticus is structured.

28. Some Bible translations render the word "commandment" in its singular form to make it seem that Moses is referring to just one commandment. But as Eugene Merrill points out in *The New American Commentary: Deuteronomy* on page 391, "This single word 'commandment' occurs regularly in Deuteronomy as a term denoting the entire covenant text (cf. 4:2; 5:29; 7:9; 8:2, 6; 11:8, 13, 22, 27; 13:4, 18; 15:5; 26:13, 18; 27:1; 28:1, 9, 13; 30:8)."

29. Prior to the law, there was no tabernacle or temple for God to dwell on earth with his people. When the law came, it allowed God's people to dwell with him, though they still needed to keep their distance and only the high priest could enter the most holy place of the temple once per year on the Day of Atonement. When Jesus died for our sins

and was resurrected, believers could journey even closer to the presence of God into the most holy place, though now the temple is no longer physical but heavenly (Hebrews 10:19-22; 12:18-24).

30. Frank Thielman, "Law," *Dictionary of Paul and His Letters,* eds. Gerald F. Hawthorne, Ralph P. Martin, and Daniel G. Reid (Downers Grove, IL: InterVarsity Press, 1993), 541.

Chapter 8—Are Women Second-Class Citizens?

1. Christopher Hitchens, *God Is Not Great: How Religion Poisons Everything* (New York: Twelve, 2009), 54-55.

2. Dwight M. Pratt, "Woman," *The International Standard Bible Encyclopaedia,* eds. James Orr et al. (Chicago, IL: The Howard-Severance Company, 1915), 3100.

3. F.L. Cross and Elizabeth A. Livingstone, eds., "Thecla, St.," *The Oxford Dictionary of the Christian Church* (New York: Oxford University Press, 2005), 1608.

4. For examples see Joanne Turpin, *Women in the Church* (Cincinnati, OH: St. Anthony Messenger Press, 2007) and Elizabeth Gillan Muir, *A Women's History of the Christian Church* (Toronto, Canada: University of Toronto Press, 2019).

5. *Epist. ad Vid. Jun.* i. c. 2, p. 340, as cited in Venables, Edmund. "Chrysostom, John," eds. William Smith and Henry Wace, *A Dictionary of Christian Biography, Literature, Sects and Doctrines* (London: John Murray, 1877–1887). Other translations of Libanius's exclamation might say "Good heavens! What women these Christians have!"

6. For further study, see Catherine C. Kroeger, "Women in Greco-Roman World and Judaism," *Dictionary of New Testament Background: A Compendium of Contemporary Biblical Scholarship* (Downers Grove, IL: InterVarsity Press, 2000).

7. Craig S. Keener, *Matthew,* vol. 1, The IVP New Testament Commentary Series (Downers Grove, IL: InterVarsity Press, 1997), Matthew 28:1.

8. M.J. Evans, "Women," *Dictionary of the Old Testament: Pentateuch,* eds. T. Desmond Alexander and David W. Baker (Downers Grove, IL: InterVarsity Press, 2003), 898.

9. Catherine C. Kroeger, "Women in Greco-Roman World and Judaism," *Dictionary of New Testament Background: A Compendium of Contemporary Biblical Scholarship* (Downers Grove, IL: InterVarsity Press, 2000), 1276-1277.

10. Dorothy Patterson, "Woman," *Holman Illustrated Bible Dictionary*, eds. Chad Brand et al. (Nashville, TN: Holman Bible Publishers, 2003), 1680.

11. For examples, see Jorunn Jacobsen Buckley, "An Interpretation of Logion 114 in the Gospel of Thomas," *Novum Testamentum* 27, no. 1 (1985).

12. Harry Y. Gamble, "Literacy and Book Culture," *Dictionary of New Testament Background: A Compendium of Contemporary Biblical Scholarship* (Downers Grove, IL: InterVarsity Press, 2000), 645.

13. Deuteronomy 33:7, 29; Psalms 20:2; 70:5; 89:19; 121:1-2 (2x); 124:8; 146:5; Hosea 13:9.

14. Robert L. Saucy, "Paul's Teaching on the Ministry of Women," in *Women and Men in Ministry: A Complementary Perspective*, eds. Robert L. Saucy and Judith K. TenElshof (Chicago, IL: Moody Press, 2001).

15. For examples, see Matthew 26:39, John 6:38, and 1 Corinthians 15:28.

16. Jesus claimed equality with God in John 10:30, John 14:9-11, and elsewhere.

17. William Arndt et al., *A Greek-English Lexicon of the New Testament and Other Early Christian Literature* (Chicago, IL: University of Chicago Press, 2000), s.v. "ἀδελφός".

18. William Arndt et al., *A Greek-English Lexicon of the New Testament and Other Early Christian Literature*, s.v. "ἄνθρωπος."

19. See Peter Lampe, "Prisca (Person)," *The Anchor Yale Bible Dictionary*, ed. David Noel Freedman (New York: Doubleday, 1992), 468. Some scholars have even suggested that Priscilla is the author of the book of Hebrews. Its strange lack of authorship might be due to the fact that it was written by a woman who didn't want her work to be disregarded among men. But this is not conclusive, and few scholars hold to Priscilla as a likely candidate.

20. D.A. Carson, *The Gospel According to John*, The Pillar New Testament Commentary (Grand Rapids, MI: InterVarsity Press, 1991), 227.

21. Some translations emphasize the "man" as being the image bearer of God, but the Hebrew word for "man" is often used to describe all humanity. The use of "male and female" in the same verse implies that inclusion of both sexes is the correct way to understand it. For further study on this subject, see Maryanne Cline Horowitz, "The Image of God in Man: Is Woman Included?" *The Harvard Theological Review* 72 (3/4).

22. Allen C. Myers, *The Eerdmans Bible Dictionary* (Grand Rapids, MI: Eerdmans, 1987), 747.

23. Naomi defended her name as "bitter" in Ruth 1:21. But Ruth 1:22 begins with "So Naomi…"

24. See the genealogy of Jesus in Matthew 1.

Chapter 9—Turning Up the Heat on Eternal Destiny

1. Nora Barlow, ed., *The Autobiography of Charles Darwin* (New York: Collins, 1958), http://darwin-online.org.uk/content/frameset?pageseq=1&itemID=F1497&viewtype=text.

2. Ralph E. Powell, "Hell," *Baker Encyclopedia of the Bible,* ed. Walter A. Elwell (Grand Rapids, MI: Baker, 1988), 954.

3. Francis Chan and Preston Sprinkle, *Erasing Hell: What God Said About Eternity and the Things We Made Up* (Colorado Springs, CO: David C. Cook, 2011), 13.

4. See Matthew 25:41 and Revelation 20:10.

5. The KJV often translates the Hebrew "Sheol" as hell, but they are not the same thing.

6. "Gehenna," *Baker Encyclopedia of the Bible,* ed. Walter A. Elwell (Grand Rapids, MI: Baker, 1988).

7. See Revelation 20:10 and 21:8; Matthew 5:22; 13:30, 40-33; 25:41; Mark 9:43-48; Luke 15:6.

8. According to Thomas Oden in his *Systematic Theology* page 452, "There is no scriptural-ecumenical authority for the view that metaphors like the fire and the worm must be taken literally." We shall see further on that major evangelical heavyweight theologians such as J. I. Packer and others also hold to the figurative approach.

9. J. I. Packer, *Concise Theology: A Guide to Historic Christian Beliefs* (Wheaton, IL: Tyndale, 1993), 262.

10. Quoted from Lee Strobel, *The Case for Faith: A Journalist Investigates the Toughest Objections to Christianity* (Grand Rapids, MI: Zondervan, 2000), 174.

11. "Self-injury/cutting," Mayo Clinic, December 07, 2018, accessed August 23, 2020, https://www.mayoclinic.org/diseases-conditions/self-injury/symptoms-causes/syc-20350950.

12. J.I. Packer, *Concise Theology: A Guide to Historic Christian Beliefs* (Wheaton, IL: Tyndale, 1993), 262-263.

13. Quoted from Jim Gabour, "A Katrina Survivor's Tale: 'They Forgot Us and That's When Things Started to Get Bad,'" *The Guardian*, August 27, 2015, sec. US news, https://www.theguardian.com/us-news/2015/aug/27/katrina-survivors-tale-they-up-and-forgot-us.

14. Ralph E. Powell, "Hell," *Baker Encyclopedia of the Bible*, Walter A. Elwell (Grand Rapids, MI: Baker, 1988), 954.

15. C.S. Lewis, *The Great Divorce*, from The C.S. Lewis Signature Classics (San Francisco, CA: HarperOne, 2017), 504.

16. See Jeremiah 1:5.

17. J. Dudley Woodberry, Russell G. Shubin, and G. Marks, "Why Muslims Convert," ChristianityToday.com, accessed November 25, 2020, https://www.christianitytoday.com/ct/2007/october/42.80.html. According to the survey presented in the article, "More than one in four respondents, 27 percent, noted dreams and visions before their decision for Christ, 40 percent at the time of conversion, and 45 percent afterward."

18. See Matthew 25:14-30. See also Matthew 16:27 and 2 Corinthians 5:10.

19. Ralph E. Powell, "Hell," *Baker Encyclopedia of the Bible*, Walter A. Elwell (Grand Rapids, MI: Baker, 1988), 955.

20. C.S. Lewis, *The Great Divorce*, from The C.S. Lewis Signature Classics (San Francisco, CA: HarperOne, 2017). 506.

21. The sermon is "Sinners in the Hands of an Angry God" by the theologian Jonathan Edwards, preached during America's First Great Awakening in Enfield, Connecticut, 1741. This message was directed to the church, and many have called it the most famous sermon ever preached in America.

22. See 2 Corinthians 5:11-21.

23. Isaiah 6:5.

Chapter 10—Why Would God Kill His Own Son?

1. Steven Pinker, *The Better Angels of Our Nature: Why Violence Has Declined* (New York: Penguin, 2012). 134.

2. R.C. Sproul, *The Holiness of God* (Carol Stream, IL: Tyndale, 1998).

3. Stanley Milgram, "Behavioral Study of Obedience," *Journal of Abnormal & Social Psychology* 67, no. 4 (October 1963): 371-78.

4. Milgram, "Behavioral Study of Obedience," 375.

5. Cornelius Plantinga Jr., *Not the Way It's Supposed to Be: A Breviary of Sin* (Grand Rapids, MI: Eerdmans, 1996), 176.

6. See Matthew 23:27-28.

7. Gerald P. Cowen, "Heart," *Holman Illustrated Bible Dictionary,* eds. Chad Brand et al. (Nashville, TN: Holman, 2003), 731.

8. "Times Square 'mugger' held on murder charges in NJ nurse death," Kevin Sheehan, Reuven Fenton, Tina Moore and Jorge Fitz-Gibbon. Newyorkpost.com, October 10, 2021, https://nypost.com/2021/10/10/man-faces-murder-charges-after-nurse-dies-amid-nyc-mugging/. Accessed October 12, 2021. "Manhattan judge frees alleged looter busted in bloody attack on NYPD cop," Larry Celona and Bruce Golding, Newyorkpost.com, https://nypost.com/2020/06/12/nyc-judge-frees-alleged-looter-accused-in-bloody-attack-on-nypd-cop/. Accessed October 12, 2021.

9. For more on the biblical case for the retributive theory of justice, See Craig, *Atonement and the Death of Christ: An Exegetical, Historical, and Philosophical Exploration* (Waco, TX: Baylor University Press, 2020), 175.

10. Craig, *Atonement and the Death of Christ,* 178.

11. Craig, *Atonement and the Death of Christ,* 188-189.

12. Craig presents at least five reasons in his book *Atonement and the Death of Christ.*

Epilogue: Good News from a Good God

1. A.W. Tozer, *The Knowledge of the Holy: The Attributes of God, Their Meaning in the Christian Life* (San Francisco, CA: Harper & Row, 1978), 1.

Serving others until the whole world hears about Jesus.

Josh McDowell
A CRU MINISTRY

- jmministry
- josh_mcdowell
- joshmcdowellministry
- JoshMcDowell
- jmmespanol

Visit **www.josh.org** for articles, discussion guides, videos, devotionals, and other resources to help you share the story of God's love.

Matthew Tingblad

▶ @achristianperspective
◎ matthewtingblad
ⓕ Matthew Tingblad

To learn more about
Matthew, visit:

josh.org/matthew

Josh McDowell
A CRU MINISTRY